# MILLIKEN'S

# COMPLETE BOOK OF

# Instant Activities

## Over **110** Reproducibles for Today's Differentiated Classroom

Author: Deborah Kopka
Cover design: Logo Design Team
Page Layout: Kati Baker

Printed in the United States of America

ISBN 978-1-4291-1472-1

MILLIKEN
P.O. Box 802 • Dayton, OH 45401
www.LorenzEducationalPress.com

## How to Use This Book . . .

The activities in this book provide an excellent source of instant, cross-curricular practice for elementary students. The pages can be used as drill reinforcement or as independent instructional material and are designed to help motivate students to learn through a variety of exercises. The activities in this book are grouped by skill; these skills may overlap more than one grade level and should be used in ways that best meet each student's needs. The reproducibles are created so that a student can work with a minimum of supervision in a classroom or at home. Additional practice and teacher information can be found in the charts at the beginning of each section. Answer keys have been provided in the back of the book.

 EXTRA! EXTRA! When you see this symbol, be sure to check out the "extra" extension activity provided.

## Table of Contents

# Language Arts

The 28 Language Arts activities in this section will reinforce your students' understanding of English language conventions (grammar, punctuation, spelling, capitalization, and writing complete sentences). They will also use descriptive words, read and comprehend narrative passages, organize material, and improve their printing skills. Depending on your class level and where you are in your curriculum, students may give answers orally or in writing. You may also choose to pair non-native English speakers with native English speakers to work together on the activities.

| Activity Title | Page | Content Standard and Skills Reinforced | Extension Activities |
|---|---|---|---|
| Write the Lowercase Letter | 5 | Lowercase letters | Cover your classroom alphabet for this activity. When students have finished the activity sheet, point to items in the classroom and have them write the lowercase letter that begins the word for each item. |
| Help the Bear Get Home | 6 | •Uppercase letters<br>•Lowercase letters | Cover your classroom alphabet for this activity. When students have finished the activity sheet, dictate various letters for them to write on a separate piece of paper, calling out uppercase and lowercase at random. |
| Days of the Week | 7 | •Capitalization<br>•Identifying days of the week<br>•Printing legibly | Dictate sentences and have students fill in any day of the week they choose. Examples: Next _____, I will see my friends. On _____, it might be sunny. |
| Months of the Year | 8 | •Capitalization<br>•Identifying months of the year<br>•Printing legibly | Call out various monthly occurrences or holidays that all students know—Valentine's Day, New Year's Day, Independence Day, Thanksgiving—and have students write the month in which it occurs. |
| Where Are the Capital Letters? | 9 | •Capitalization<br>•Reading a narrative passage | Choose a simple narrative paragraph from current class reading, and write it on the board in lowercase letters only. Have students rewrite the paragraph, capitalizing words as necessary. |
| Spelling Word Scramble | 10 | •Grade 1 high-frequency word recognition<br>•Vocabulary development | Write several scrambled words from the grade 1 high-frequency list on the board (without giving students a word box of terms to refer to), including: *are, big, do, give, if, old, put, red, they, with.* Have them write the unscrambled words on a separate sheet of paper. |
| Beginning Blends | 11 | •Matching images to printed words<br>•Initial consonant blends | Before students begin this activity, review that blends of consonants can occur at the beginning of words. After the activity, have students generate a word with these initial blends: *dr (dress), fl (flag), pr (print), sk (skip), sl (sled), sm (smile).* |
| Ending Blends | 12 | •Matching images to printed words<br>•Ending consonant blends | Before students begin this activity, review that blends of consonants can occur at the ends of words. After the activity, have students generate several words for the ending blend *nd (band, end, find, friend, kind, pond,* and *end).* |
| It Rhymes! | 13 | •Matching rhyming words<br>•Printing legibly | Have students think of rhyming words for *fire, goose, jam, jet, paw,* and *snake.* |
| What's the First Letter? | 14 | Distinguishing initial consonant sounds in single-syllable words | Have students distinguish the initial consonant sound for *fall, fence, gourd, head, leaf, rock,* and *wish.* Have students distinguish the initial consonant sound for two-syllable items in your classroom. |
| What's the Last Letter? | 15 | Distinguishing final consonant sounds in single-syllable words | Have students distinguish the final consonant sound for *chip, dream, flip, job, light, room, shout,* and *soon.* Have students distinguish the final consonant sound for two-syllable items in your classroom. |
| Match the Vowel Sound | 16 | •Recognition of short-vowel sound and long-vowel sound<br>•Reading a narrative passage | Review that when you hear long *e* in the middle of a word, it's usually spelled with *ee* or *ea.* Write each student's name on the board and have the class identify the vowel sounds in each name. |
| Make New Words | 17 | Reading/constructing compound words | Reverse the activity. Give students these compound words and have them draw pictures to create an equation, as in the activity: *basketball, lipstick, playground, raincoat, sailboat, shoelace, snowball, sunlight.* |

| | | | |
|---|---|---|---|
| Contractions | 18 | Contractions | Additional contraction equations for students to solve include: *can + not; what + is; will + not; does + not; is + not; she + is; you + will; he + will.* |
| Plurals | 19 | Plurals formed by adding *s* | Draw another caterpillar on the board with these words in the body parts: *bird, book, car, chair, hat, paper, pencil,* and *table.* Have students form the plurals by adding *s* and generate a sentence for each word. |
| Possessives | 20 | Possessives ending in *'s* with singular nouns | Review the items with students; some may have more than one answer. Generate additional sentences about items in your classroom or in the school. Example: "That teacher's students are learning about clouds." |
| Where Does This Animal Belong? | 21 | •Categorizing<br>•One-, two-, and three-syllable words<br>•Printing legibly | Review the spelling of each animal name, particularly the three-syllable words. Ask students in which category each of these belongs: *cat, crocodile, elephant, dog, chicken, flamingo, lion,* and *tiger.* |
| My Favorites! | 22 | •Categorizing<br>•Printing legibly | Have students generate additional categories, such as *My Friends, My Family,* or *My Favorite Colors.* Have more advanced students classify the items in each category (example: types of food in the *Food* category). |
| What Comes Next? | 23 | •Story sequencing<br>•Predicting | After students give the correct sequence for each set of images, have them predict what might be in the fourth panel for each character featured. |
| Which Picture Doesn't Belong? | 24 | Story sequencing | After students give the correct sequence, have them add another picture for each sequence that might be a probable event in the sequence. Have them write this event in a simple sentence. Example: The children go back to class. |
| Solve the Mystery | 25 | •Making deductions<br>•Predicting | Review the meaning of making a deduction from facts presented in a story. Discuss what clues in each story led students to draw their conclusions about what happened. Have students make a prediction about what each character will do in each story. |
| Who? What? When? Where? How? | 26 | Comprehending text by answering *who, what, when, where,* and *how* questions | Ask students additional *who, what, when, where,* and *how* questions about this simple story and allow them to make up answers: Who is Juana? What was she doing before she heard the cat? When could this story have taken place? Where does Juana live? How did Juana open the door? |
| Cause and Effect | 27 | Cause and effect | Review cause and effect before handing out this activity. Accept all answers when reviewing the activity. Pose other cause statements and have students write or orally give the effect. Examples: "I turned on the classroom lights." "She filled the dog's food bowl." You can also have students act out a cause-and-effect situation. |
| Sentence Starters | 28 | Writing coherent sentences | Generate several more sentence starters and write them on the board. You can use sentence starters in any content area to ask students what they know, what they want to learn more about, etc. |
| Words That Describe | 29 | Using descriptive words | Point to common items in your classroom, pictures in current classroom reading, or things students see through your classroom windows. Have students generate descriptive words for each item. |
| Describe a Friend | 30 | Using descriptive words | Draw a graphic organizer on the board that is identical to the one in the activity. Draw a simple picture of a person in the center circle that students will all know—this could be you, your school's principal, a famous actor, a singer, etc. Have students call out descriptive words to complete the organizer. Add as many circles as necessary. |
| What If You Could Fly? | 31 | •Writing a narrative response to a story starter<br>•Predicting<br>•Writing coherent sentences | Pose other "what if" questions for which students could write a narrative response. Examples: "What if we all looked the same?" "What if it never got dark?" "What if your pet could talk?" "What if we all spoke a different language?" Ask students to generate a few of their own "what if" questions. |
| Tanya's Furry Gift | 32 | •Reading a narrative passage<br>•Using context to understand words | Have students answer *who, what, when, where, why,* and *how* questions about this passage. Who was going to buy Tanya a puppy? What is the special occasion? When were they going to buy the puppy? Where is the puppy? Why did Tanya go back to bed? How did Tanya hug the puppy? |

# Write the Lowercase Letter

Write the matching lowercase letter in each balloon.

a b c d e f g h i j k l m n o p q r s t u v w x y z

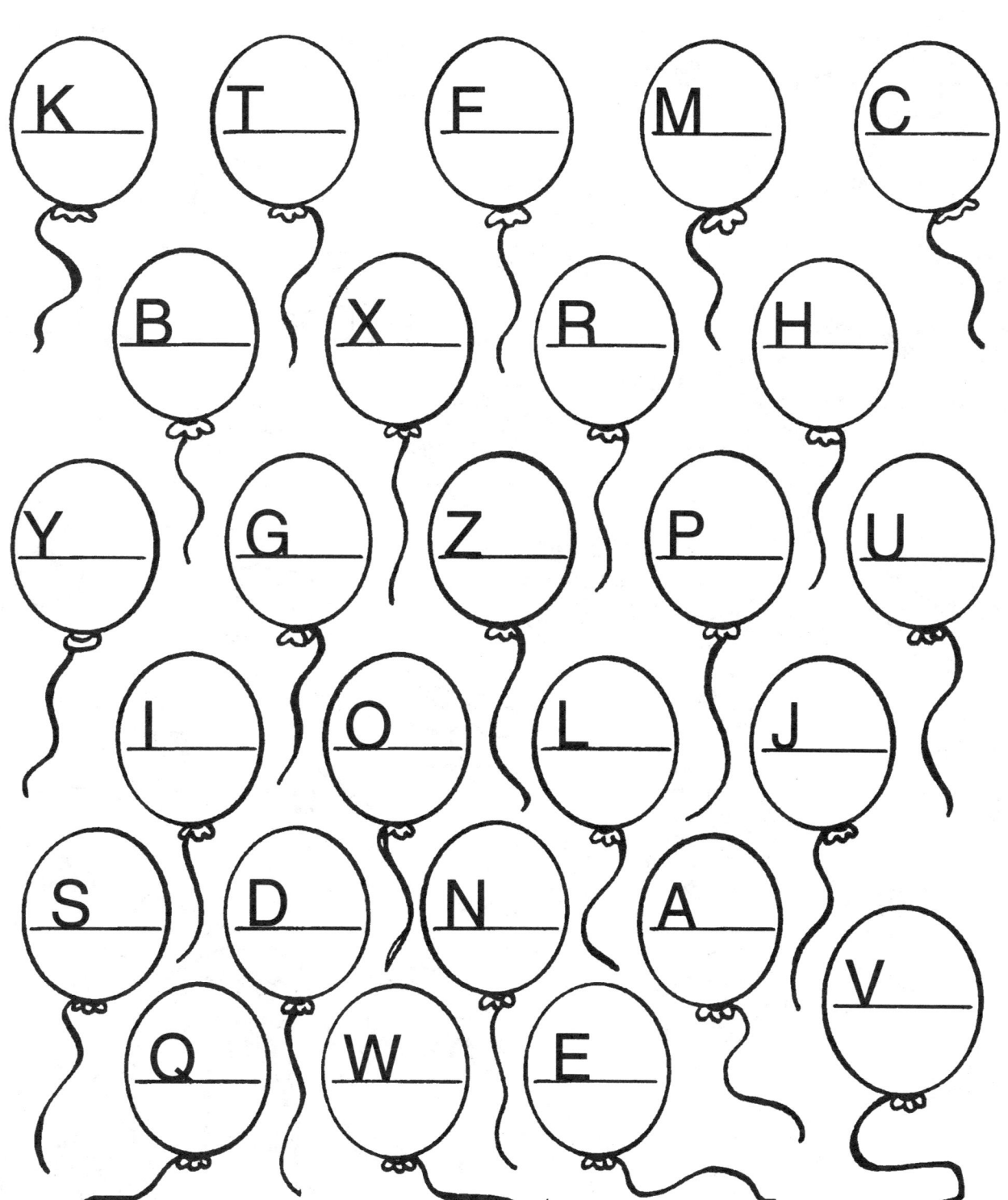

**5**

# Help the Bear Get Home

Help the bear get home!  Color the uppercase letters orange.
Color the lowercase letters green.

# Days of the Week

Write the days of the week in order.
Start each one with a **capital letter**.

wednesday     friday     saturday     monday
sunday     tuesday     thursday

1. _____

2. _____

3. _____

4. _____

5. _____

6. _____

7. _____

# Months of the Year

Practice writing the months of the year.  Trace each word.

1. January

2. February

3. March

4. April

5. May

6. June

7. July

8. August

9. September

10. October

11. November

12. December

# Where Are the Capital Letters?

Circle each letter that should be capitalized.

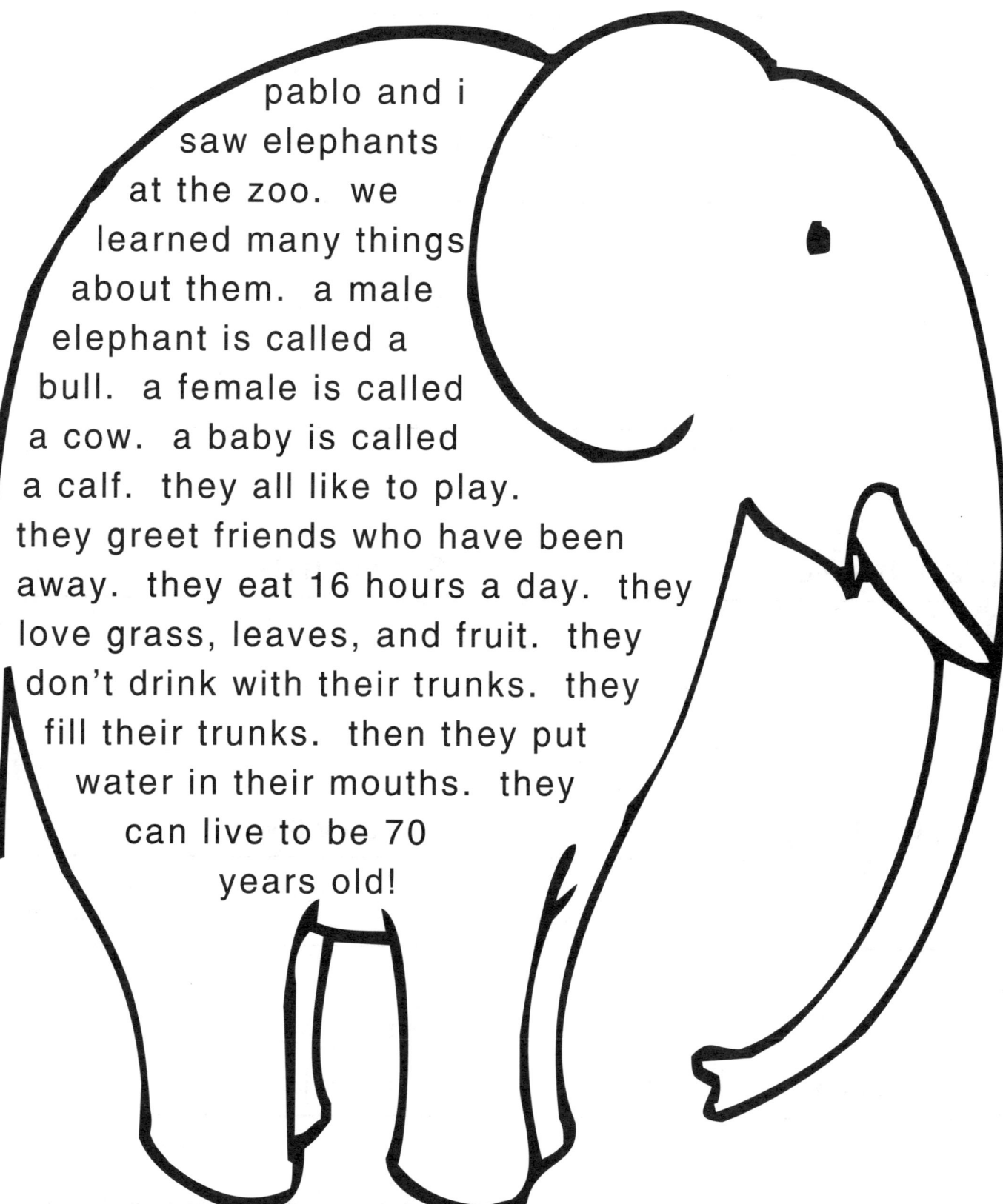

pablo and i
saw elephants
at the zoo.  we
learned many things
about them.  a male
elephant is called a
bull.  a female is called
a cow.  a baby is called
a calf.  they all like to play.
they greet friends who have been
away.  they eat 16 hours a day.  they
love grass, leaves, and fruit.  they
don't drink with their trunks.  they
fill their trunks.  then they put
water in their mouths.  they
can live to be 70
years old!

Language Arts

# Spelling Word Scramble

Unscramble these words.

| down | jump | little | yellow |
| always | friend | house | light |

1. h g l i t

_____

_ _ _ _ _ _ _ _ _ _ _ _ _ _ _ _

_____

2. u h s e o

_____

_ _ _ _ _ _ _ _ _ _ _ _ _ _ _ _

_____

3. w o l l e y

_____

_ _ _ _ _ _ _ _ _ _ _ _ _ _ _ _

_____

4. t t l l i e

_____

_ _ _ _ _ _ _ _ _ _ _ _ _ _ _ _

_____

5. w o n d

_____

_ _ _ _ _ _ _ _ _ _ _ _ _ _ _ _

_____

6. i e f r n d

_____

_ _ _ _ _ _ _ _ _ _ _ _ _ _ _ _

_____

7. a a l y s w

_____

_ _ _ _ _ _ _ _ _ _ _ _ _ _ _ _

_____

8. p u m j

_____

_ _ _ _ _ _ _ _ _ _ _ _ _ _ _ _

_____

# Beginning Blends

Look at each picture.  Circle the word that **begins** with the same sound.

| | | | |
|---|---|---|---|
| brush | bread | book | bucket |
| clown | kite | click | cat |
| glass | girl | gift | glow |
| grass | green | giraffe | glass |
| plant | pants | paint | play |
| snail | soft | snake | sail |
| stop | start | soft | sat |
| tree | tent | truck | ten |

# Ending Blends

Look at each picture.  Circle the word that **ends** with the same sound.

| ant | pen | arm | tent |
| crown | green | clown | swan |
| desk | ask | dear | date |
| hand | sand | pan | pony |
| song | long | site | swallow |
| stamp | lamb | lamp | street |
| stick | clip | click | string |
| swing | wing | swat | swipe |

# It Rhymes!

Write the word beside each picture. Draw a line to the word
that **rhymes** with it.

 _____

 _____

 _____

 _____

 _____

 _____

 _____

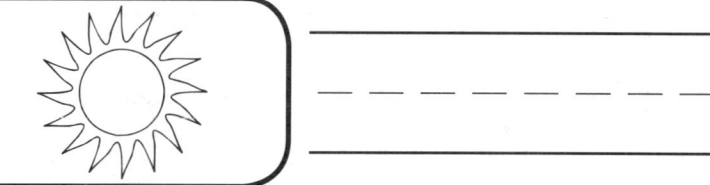 _____

A. hose

B. wish

C. train

D. tail

E. house

F. fun

G. pear

H. bake

# What's the First Letter?

| | | | |
|---|---|---|---|
| ump | ock | ask | urse |
| ase | afe | arn | ake |
| all | art | ice | oot |
| ate | orse | ent | ig |

# What's the Last Letter?

| | | | |
|---|---|---|---|
| bar | co | do | chai |
| be | sou | foo | rai |
| bu | ca | ca | boa |
| doo | bea | bu | shee |

# Match the Vowel Sound

Write each word in the bubble with its vowel sound.

| pan | dime |
|-----|------|
| top | June |
| vest | tape |
| hose | big |
| lunch | meat |

# Make New Words

Write the word for each picture.  Then put both words together and write the compound word.

## *Example:*

 +  = pancake

1.  + 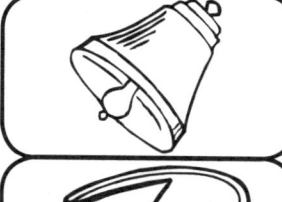 = _____

2.  +  = _____

3.  +  = _____

4.  +  = _____

5. 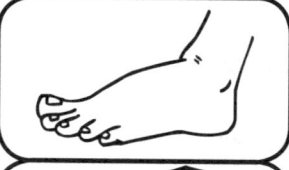 +  = _____

6.  + 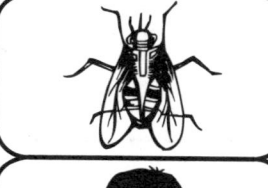 = _____

7. 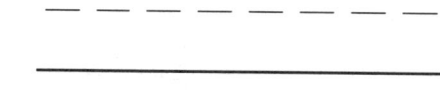 +  = _____

8.  + _____ = _____

# Contractions

Cut out the contractions at the bottom of the page.  Paste them where they belong.

1. I + am =

2. did + not =

3. she + is =

4. I + will =

5. it + is =

6. we + are =

7. do + not =

8. they + are =

- - - - - - - - ✂ - - - - - - - - - - - - - - - - - - - - - - - - - - -

| they're | we're | don't | I'm |
|---------|-------|-------|-----|
| it's | didn't | I'll | she's |

# Plurals

Add an **s** to each word in the caterpillar.  Write the correct word in each sentence.

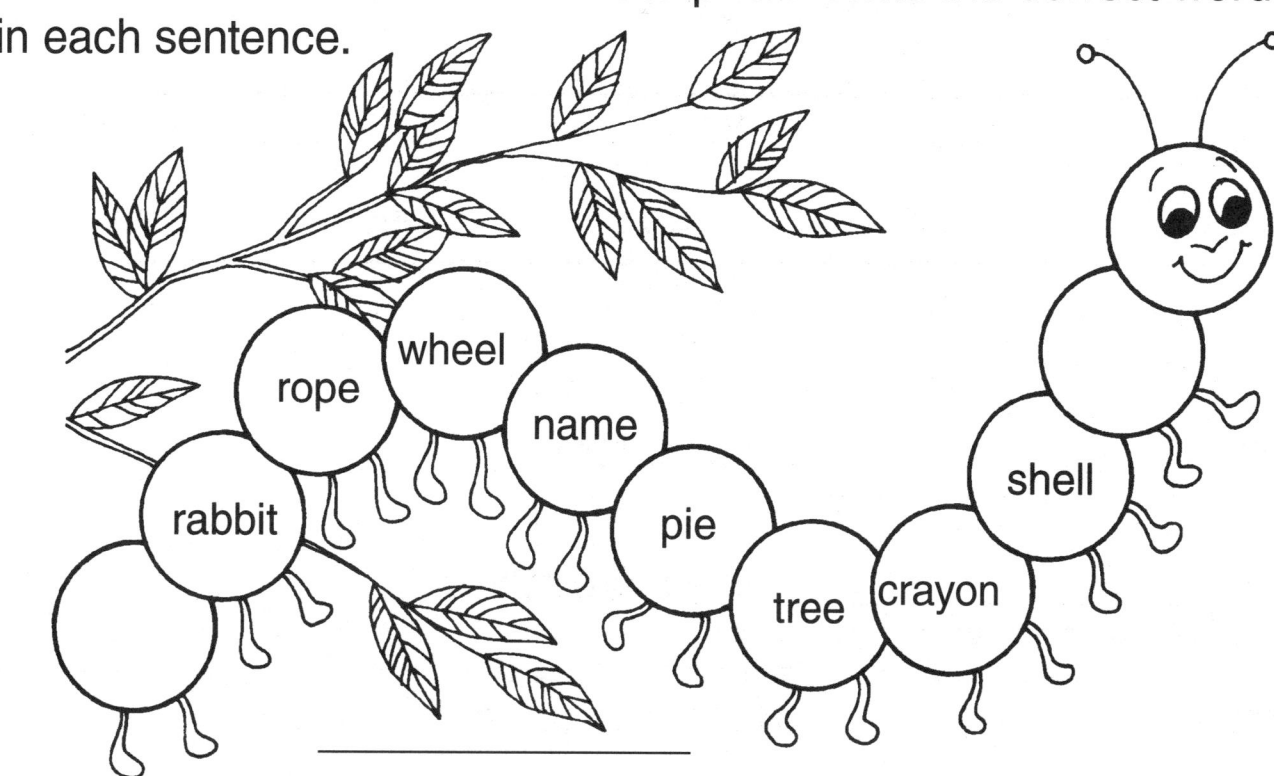

1. What are the _____ of your pets?

2. I saw many _____ on the beach.

3. All of the _____ hopped away.

4. Let's have a picnic under those _____ .

5. We use _____ to color pictures.

6. A wagon has four _____ .

7. Angie baked two apple _____ today.

8. Mona put two jump _____ in the closet.

# Possessives

Write the correct word in the space.

| tree's | dog's | horse's | cat's | giraffe's |
|--------|-------|---------|-------|-----------|
| shark's | book's | turtle's | cake's | flower's |

1. My _____ cover is torn.

2. The _____ leaves are falling.

3. My _____ bone was under the couch.

4. She cleaned her _____ hooves.

5. Our _____ kittens are tiny.

6. A _____ neck is long.

7. The _____ teeth are sharp.

8. A _____ shell is hard.

9. The birthday _____ icing was pink.

10. That _____ petals are pink.

# Where Does This Animal Belong?

Below are eight animals.  Write the name of each animal.
Then paste the animal in its box.

| **Zoo** | **Farm** |
|---|---|
| | |

# My Favorites!

Draw or write three things in each box.

**My Favorite Toys**

**My Favorite Foods**

# What Comes Next?

Write 1, 2, or 3 on each line to put the pictures in order.  Color the pictures.

# Which Picture Doesn't Belong?

Cross out the picture that does not belong.  Write 1, 2, or 3 on each line to put the remaining pictures in order. Color the pictures.

# Solve the Mystery

Write what happened in each story.

Kamal moved into his new house on Pine Street. The houses on the street look alike. Kamal ran home after his first day in his new school. He opened the front door. The rugs were different! The couch was different! The pictures on the wall were different! "When did we get these new things?" he thought.

**What happened?**

_____

_____

Mr. Kim finished his meal. He took a coat from the coat rack. He put it on. Then he went to the parking lot. He pulled car keys from his pocket. But he could not open his car door.

**What happened?**

_____

_____

# Who? What? When? Where? How?

Read this story.  Then answer the questions.

It was late in the day after school. Juana had just come home. She heard a meow. She opened the front door. There sat a small cat! She petted it gently. It purred and purred.

1. Who heard a meow?

_____
_ _ _ _ _ _ _ _ _ _ _ _ _ _ _ _
_____

2. What did Juana open?

_____
_ _ _ _ _ _ _ _ _ _ _ _ _ _ _ _
_____

3. When did this happen?

_____
_ _ _ _ _ _ _ _ _ _ _ _ _ _ _ _
_____

4. Where did this happen?

_____
_ _ _ _ _ _ _ _ _ _ _ _ _ _ _ _
_____

5. How did Juana pet the cat?

_____

# Cause and Effect

Each cause leads to an effect. Look at the causes in the left-hand column. What happens as a result?

| CAUSE | EFFECT |
|-------|--------|
| Tom opens the window. | |
| It starts to rain. | |
| The squirrel digs for acorns. | |
| The day got warmer and warmer. | |

**27**

# Sentence Starters

Finish the sentences.

_____

- - - - - - - - - - - -

1. I like to _____ .

_____

- - - - - - - - - - - -

2. At home, I _____ .

_____

- - - - - - - - - - - -

3. I get angry when _____ .

_____

- - - - - - - - - - - -

4. I like my favorite sport because _____ .

_____

- - - - - - - - - - - -

5. On a sunny day, I _____ .

_____

- - - - - - - - - - - -

6. On a rainy day, I _____ .

_____

- - - - - - - - - - - -

7. One thing I learned today is _____ .

_____

- - - - - - - - - - - -

8. Next week, I will _____ .

# Words That Describe

Draw a line from each picture to a word that describes it.

1.

**A. fluffy**

2.

**B. long**

3.

**C. shady**

4.

**D. juicy**

5.

**E. happy**

6.

**F. warm**

7.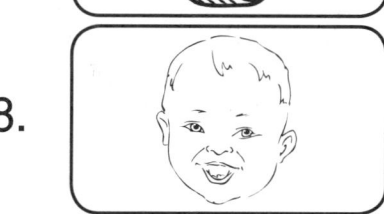

**G. round**

8.

**H. striped**

# Describe a Friend

Draw one of your friends in the center circle.  Write a word that describes the person in each small circle.

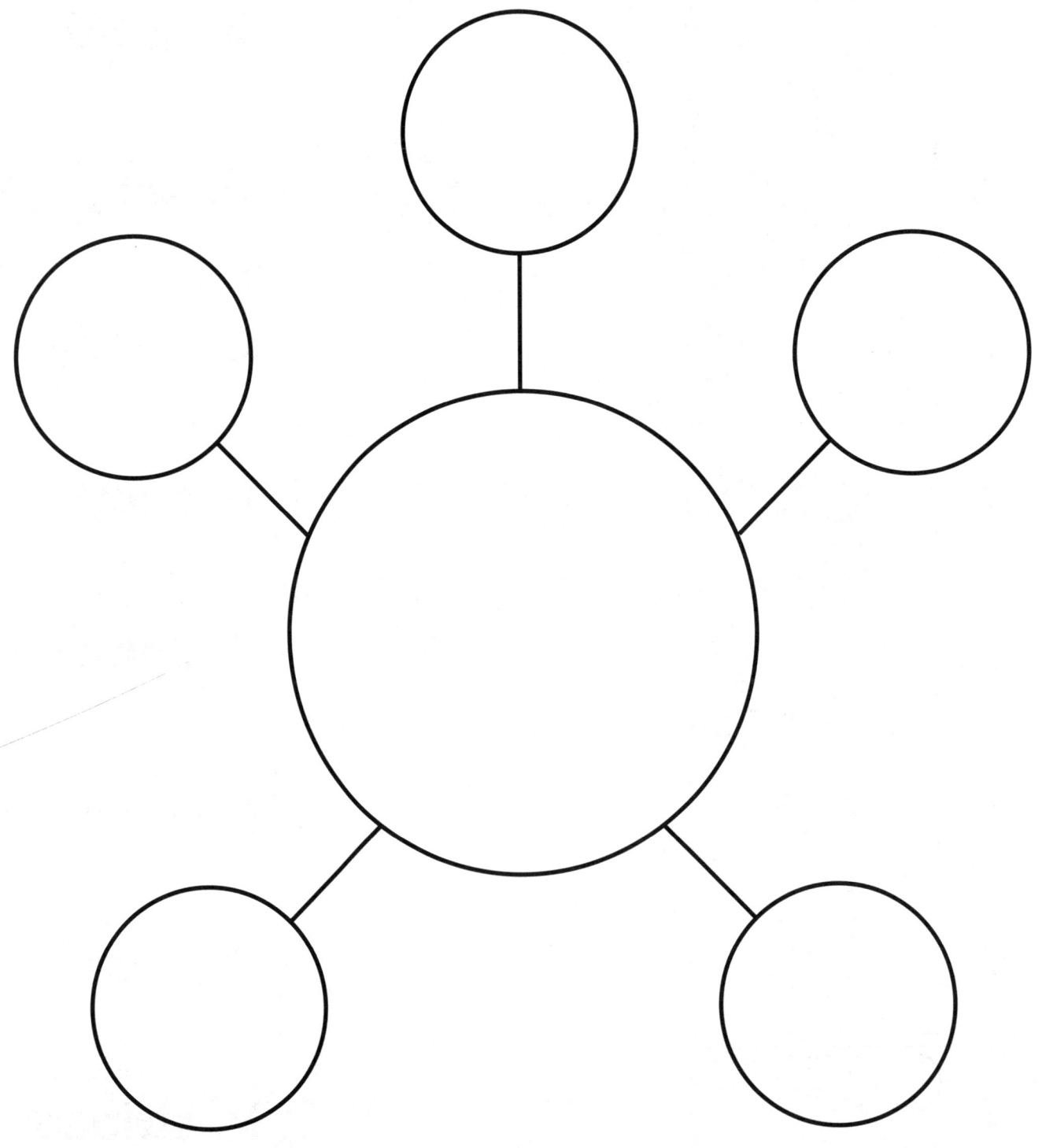

# What If You Could Fly?

Imagine you could fly!  Where would you go?  What would you
want to see?  Write what you would do if you could fly.  Then
draw a picture.

_____

- - - - - - - - - - - - - - - - - - - - - - - - - - - -

_____
_____

- - - - - - - - - - - - - - - - - - - - - - - - - - - -

_____
_____

- - - - - - - - - - - - - - - - - - - - - - - - - - - -

_____

# Tanya's Furry Gift

Fill in each blank with one of the words below.

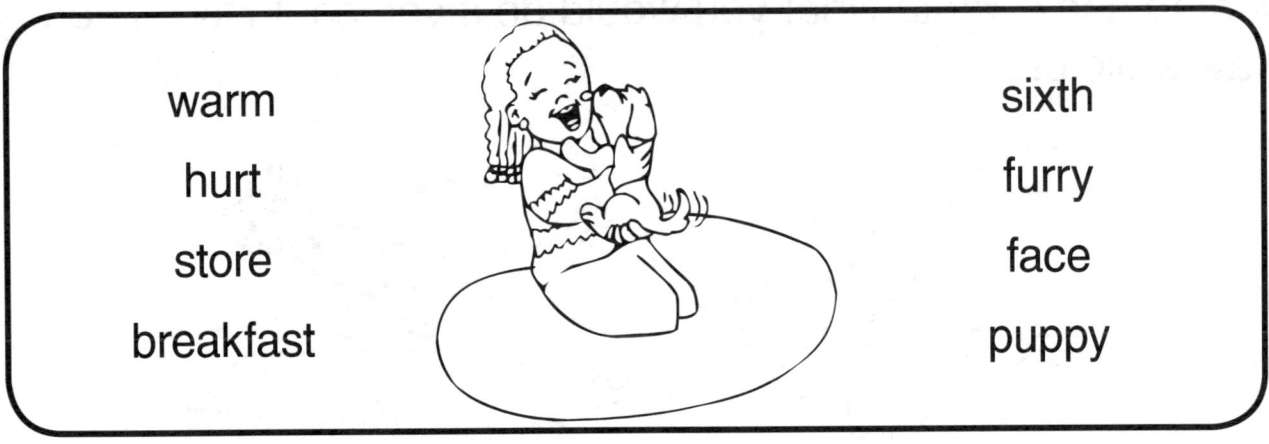

warm

hurt

store

breakfast

sixth

furry

face

puppy

Today was Tanya's big day!  It was her _____ birthday.

Her dad was going to take her to the pet _____ .  They

were going to pick out a puppy.  Tanya went down to breakfast.  Her

mom had fixed her favorite _____ .  Tanya began to eat.

But her throat _____ .  She felt hot.  "You're not well!"

said her mom.  "You should go back to bed."  So Tanya did.  A little

later, she woke up.  Something _____ and _____

was licking her _____ .  Her dad stood at the end of the

bed.  "Happy birthday, Tanya!" he said.  "Do you like your new

_____ ?"  Tanya happily hugged the puppy.

# Social Studies

The 28 Social Studies activities in this section heighten and reinforce students' awareness of their local and global communities. Students will:
- Identify cultural traditions
- Read a simple map and identify cardinal directions
- Recognize notable U.S. presidents, symbols, landmarks, and citizens
- Understand basic economic concepts of goods, services, producers, and consumers
- Appreciate the diversity of our communities and our nation

| Activity Title | Page | Content Standard and Skills Reinforced | EXTRA! Extension Activities |
|---|---|---|---|
| Our Classroom Rules | 36 | •Reasons for rules<br>•Classroom rules | Review the reasons for rules. Ask students what it would be like if we had no rules. Then review your classroom rules. Have students print them on the sheet. Encourage students to keep this sheet in their notebooks or in another place where they will see it often. |
| The Golden Rule | 37 | Respect for others | Write the Golden Rule on the board, and do this activity with the class. Have students brainstorm other examples of the Golden Rule, both in school and in their communities. These can include forgiveness, being friendly, being helpful, and not criticizing. Have students add the Golden Rule to their first activity sheet, Our Classroom Rules. |
| What I Like to Do | 38 | •Community awareness<br>•Community connectedness in the classroom | Discuss the concept of community—it includes the people and the physical establishments that create a it. Stress the fact that we all enrich each other with our skills and the happiness that comes from doing things we like to do. Post students' pictures around the classroom or on a bulletin board with the title "Our Classroom Community." Students can do this activity periodically throughout the year as they discover new things they like to do. |
| What Makes a Community? | 39 | Knowledge of and respect for the larger community | Have students talk about the establishments in their home communities and why they are important. Invite students from other cultures to discuss important places in their communities. Examples: A botánica may be an important store in a Hispanic community; a mosque is the key institution in a Muslim community; a historical society can be a major institution in a small town. |
| Urban, Rural, or Suburban? | 40 | Identifying community settings | Review the terms urban, rural, and suburban and discuss the fact that people live in these types of areas. What factors define these areas? What factors help people make choices about where they live? (Consider ways of making a living, lifestyle preferences, and transportation). |
| Jobs in My Community | 41 | Job diversity in a community | Discuss that a community is made up of many people doing different jobs that benefit all of us. Also discuss that workers usually deal with people, data (information), or things (inanimate objects such as cars). Review each of the jobs in the activity, and ask students to tell you how the person in each deals with people, data, and things. How does each of these workers help the community as a whole? |
| Tools of the Trade | 42 | Job diversity in a community | Review the various tools students have drawn, and write the jobs on the board. Post all of the activities on a bulletin board and label it "Tools of the Trade in Our Community." |
| We're All Alike! We're All Different! | 43 | •Using comparing and contrasting to discover similarities and differences<br>•Respect for diversity | Do this activity with students as a class. Have them generate similarities and differences among the students in the class, and write them on the board. Focus on principles, goals, traditions, and varied ancestry. Then have them choose the key similarities and differences to write on a graphic organizer. Discuss appreciation of the similarities and respect for the differences. Reinforce that the term respect implies tolerance. |
| What Did You Say? | 44 | Connecting idiomatic sayings to real-life experiences | Every culture has its own sayings. Many have sayings that mean the same thing as those in this activity. After you review each saying, ask students if they use similar phrases at home that mean the same thing. |

| | | | |
|---|---|---|---|
| My Favorite Holiday Tradition | 45 | Comparing and contrasting cultural traditions | Review the meaning of *tradition* before students begin this activity. When you review this activity, have students who name holidays that are not traditionally celebrated in America, such as Diwali or Day of the Dead, tell a bit about it. Use comparing and contrasting to point out similarities and differences in cultural holiday traditions. |
| My Big Events Timeline | 46 | •Sequencing and organizing information<br>•Using a timeline | Depending on the level of your students, you may need to do this activity as a whole class. Review the concepts of *events, timelines,* and *chronological order*. Identify a few recent local or national events familiar to students, and have them put the events in chronological order. Allow them to include any type of event on the timeline. Encourage them to write the time period in which the event happened. Have them put the oldest event first. |
| Things Change! | 47 | Distinguishing between past, present, and future | Do this activity as a class. Have students work together to create pictures and/or words for the way we do things now and the way we may do them in the future. Note that we still do some things today as they were done in the past—people still write letters, for example (although they probably don't use a bottle of ink and an ink pen). What other things are different now (consider the price of food, available services such as hospitals, etc.)? |
| North, South, East, or West? | 48 | •Cardinal directions<br>•Map reading | After you review this activity, introduce intermediate directions and have students find NW, NE, SW, and SE. |
| This Is My State | 49 | •Your state's relationship to other states<br>•Drawing an outline<br>•State geographic features | Point out your state on the U.S. outline map. Have students color in your state. Then have them draw an outline of your state on the bottom half of this page. Have them mark your city or town with a circle and draw in two or three key landforms and/or bodies of water. Review the cardinal and intermediate directions by asking about the location of your city relative to key state geographic features. Example: "Is our town east or west of the river?" |
| World Map Jigsaw | 50 | •Identifying the continents and oceans on a world map<br>•Correlating the information on two-dimensional maps with the information on a globe | Once students have pasted and colored the pieces of the map, work with them to label the continents, the oceans, and the cardinal directions. Point out each continent and ocean on your classroom globe. |
| United States Holidays | 51 | The significance of U.S. holidays | Review the months in which each holiday occurs. Have students tell you what other holidays they celebrate in addition to those listed. |
| The United States Flag | 52 | •The significance of the U.S. flag<br>•Flag etiquette<br>•Reading comprehension | Display your classroom U.S. flag. If possible, display a few pictures of the original U.S. flag compared to the more modern U.S. flags that have changed as new states have entered the union. Ask students what the U.S. flag represents to them. Have students from other countries describe (or draw on the board) their home-country flags and what the symbols on the flag represent. |
| The Pledge of Allegiance | 53 | The meaning of the Pledge of Allegiance | Discuss the meaning of the terms *pledge* and *allegiance*. Ask, "Why do we pledge allegiance to a flag? What does this symbolize?" |
| Symbols of the United States | 54 | U.S. symbols provide continuity and a sense of community | Discuss the significance of each symbol and, if possible, show actual pictures of them. The bald eagle is unique to the U.S. and symbolizes strength. The Liberty Bell was rung when the Declaration of Independence was signed in 1776 and on state occasions until 1846. Although cracked, it is still rung every July 4th. The Statue of Liberty represents freedom; her torch represents liberty; her tablet is inscribed with July 4, 1776; the seven rays of her crown symbolize the seas and continents. We do not know how Uncle Sam originated. He is said to be inspired by Sam Wilson, a businessman who supplied the U.S. Army with beef during the War of 1812. |
| My State Flag | 55 | •State symbols provide continuity and a sense of community<br>•Note-taking | Do this activity with the whole class. You may want to provide a line drawing of your state flag for students to copy. Or, if students can do Internet searches, have them research the flag online. Discuss each symbol on the flag. Have students write one or two words below their drawing that describes each symbol. |

| | | | |
|---|---|---|---|
| Our Elected Leaders | 56 | Familiarity with elected federal and state leaders | Have students do this activity for homework. They can get the information from their family, from TV, or from print sources, such as the newspaper. When you review this activity, make sure students have spelled the names correctly. If possible, show pictures of each of the leaders named in the activity. Discuss the role each person plays in making or enforcing laws, keeping us safe, etc. |
| The White House | 57 | •Introduction to the White House<br>•Reading a narrative passage | Ask students who have been to the White House to give their impressions of it. Ask all students what the advantages and disadvantages would be of living in such a public place, with a well-known family. |
| American Landmarks Word Search | 58 | The significance of American landmarks | Discuss the meaning of the term *landmark*. Point out the landmarks discussed in prior activities: the White House, the Statue of Liberty, and the Liberty Bell. The landmarks in this activity are also important reminders of our national history. |
| Presidents and Coins | 59 | •Identifying the presidents on U.S. coins<br>•Matching shapes | Have these coins available when you do this activity. Pass them around class. Mention other coins that are now in circulation but not as widely used, such as dollar coins. Ask students how they think the U.S. government makes decisions regarding who to put on coins. Why do we put presidents on coins? What other Americans might we put on coins? |
| Famous American Inventors | 60 | •Famous Americans<br>•Matching images to information | Discuss the fact that things are invented to fill a need in society. What needs were filled by each of these inventors? How does their work live on today? |
| Goods or Services? | 61 | Distinguishing between goods and services | Students may say that a few of these, such as bicycle shop and pet shop, supply both goods and services. Identify additional goods and services in your community or state. Identify professions that provide both goods and services—such as restaurants, gas stations, car dealerships, and movie theaters. |
| Producers or Consumers? | 62 | Distinguishing between producers and consumers | Point out common producers in your community or state, such as factories. Ask, "Who consumes this (good or service)?" Discuss that producers and consumers need each other and that people are often both producers and consumers. |
| Proud to Be You and Me! | 63 | Pride in American diversity | Discuss the term *diversity*. Ask students what they think it means to be American. Post their pictures on a bulletin board labeled "Proud to Be You and Me!" |

# Our Classroom Rules

**Rules**

Be safe

Work well with others

Be fair

Enjoy every day!

## Our Classroom Rules

_____

1. _____

_____

2. _____

_____

3. _____

_____

4. _____

_____

5. _____

# The Golden Rule

**Do unto others as you would have them do unto you.**

This means to treat other people the way you want to be treated. How are these people following the Golden Rule?

# What I Like to Do

Draw a picture of yourself doing something you like to do.  Write your name below the picture.

My name is _____ .

**38**

# What Makes a Community?

There are many things that people in a community share. Draw a line from each word to its picture.

fire department

streets

police department

school

pet store

zoo

post office

park

hospital

library

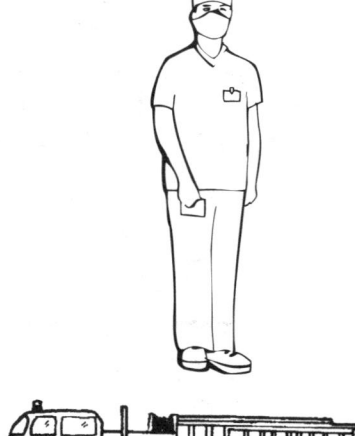

# Urban, Rural, or Suburban?

Write under each scene whether it's **urban, rural,** or **suburban**.

# Jobs in My Community

Write the name of the worker who might use each item below.

firefighter

auto mechanic

house painter

grocer

doctor

farmer

police officer

construction worker

bus driver

banker

**1.**

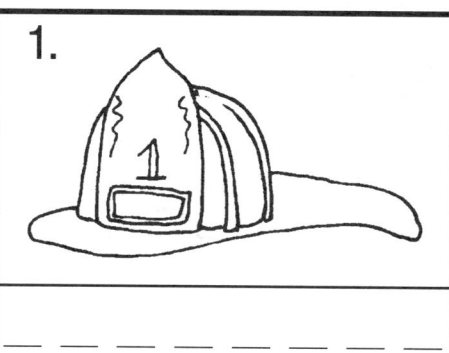

_____

**2.**

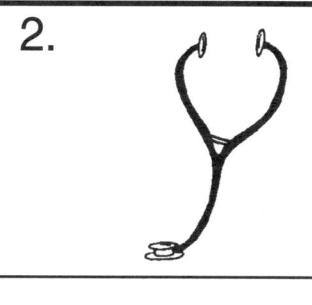

_____

**3.**

_____

**4.**

_____

**5.**

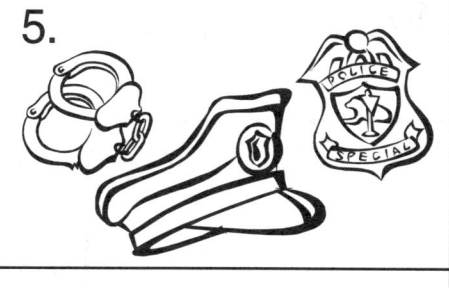

_____

**6.**

_____

**7.**

_____

**8.**

_____

**9.**

_____

**10.**

_____

Name _____  Date _____

# Tools of the Trade

Draw a tool that one of your family members uses at work.  Fill in the sentence

**Example:**

My father uses a wrench to fix cars .

My _____ uses _____ to _____ .

# We're All Alike!  We're All Different!

Write three ways that all people are alike.  Write three ways that we are different.

| How We're Alike | How We're Different |
|---|---|
| _____ | _____ |
| - - - - - - - - - | - - - - - - - - - |
| _____ | _____ |
| _____ | _____ |
| - - - - - - - - - | - - - - - - - - - |
| _____ | _____ |
| _____ | _____ |
| - - - - - - - - - | - - - - - - - - - |
| _____ | _____ |

# What Did You Say?

Draw a line from the underlined saying to its meaning.

1. I <u>see the light</u>!

2. She <u>let the cat out of the bag</u>.

3. My grandma <u>has a heart of gold</u>.

4. You <u>hit the nail on the head</u>.

5. We <u>pulled her leg</u> with that story.

6. John is <u>in the doghouse</u> for not cleaning his room.

7. I'm <u>down in the dumps</u> today.

8. He was <u>all ears</u> during class.

9. <u>There's no place like home</u>.

10. That new bike costs <u>an arm and a leg</u>.

A. Home is the best place to be.

B. feeling sad

C. really listening

D. understand

E. let out a secret

F. really got it right

G. is very kind

H. is really expensive

I. in trouble

J. fooled her

# My Favorite Holiday Tradition

Draw a picture of your favorite holiday tradition.  Then write a sentence about your picture.

_____

- - - - - - - - - - - - - - - - - - - - - - - -

_____

- - - - - - - - - - - - - - - - - - - - - - - -

_____

# My Big Events Timeline

Write or draw some big events in your life.  Put them in the order they happened.

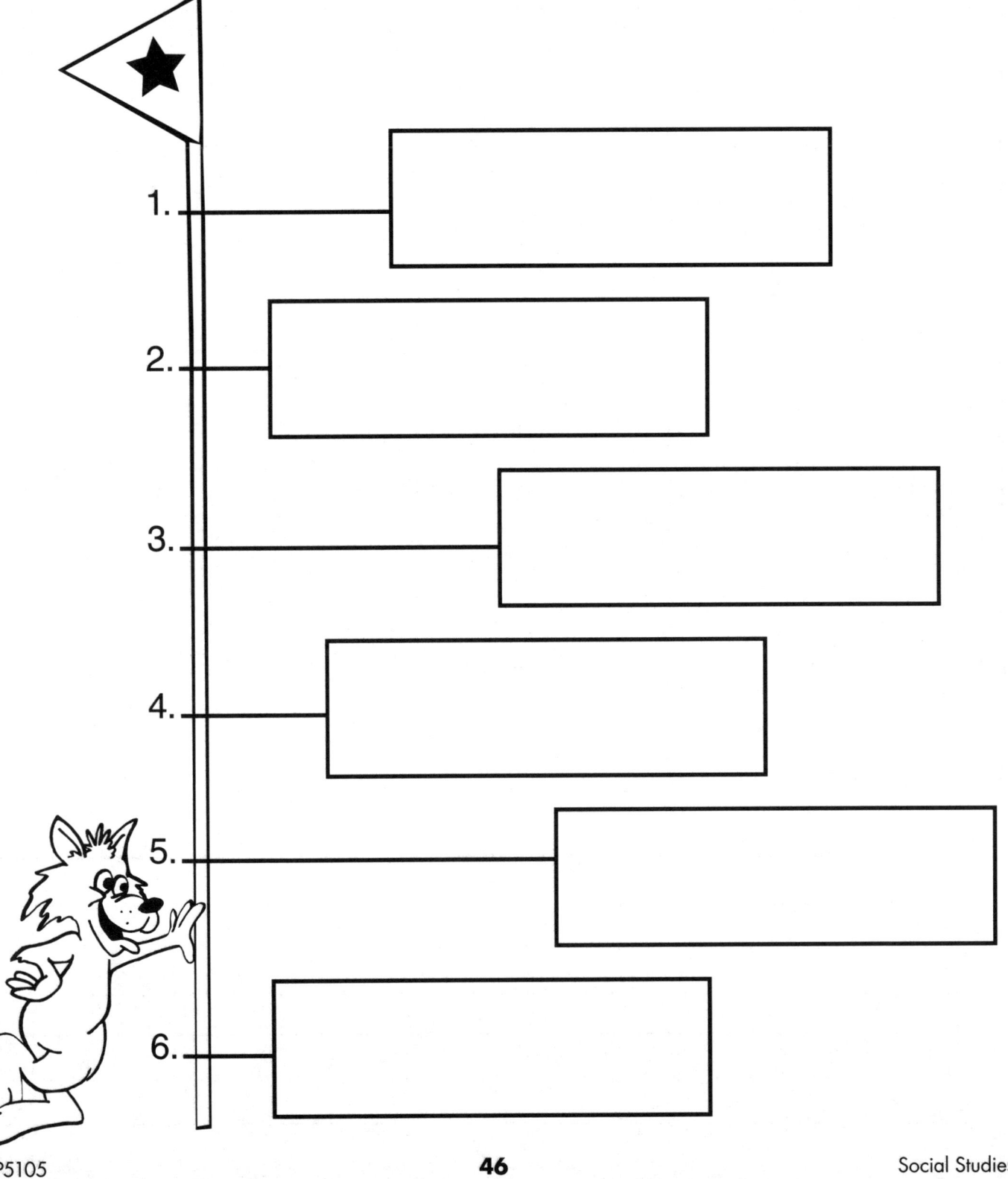

# Things Change!

Things change! Think about how we do things now. How will we do these same things in the future?

| 100 Years Ago | Today | In the Future |
|---|---|---|
|  |  |  |
|  |  |  |
|  |  |  |
|  |  |  |
|  |  |  |

# North, South, East, or West?

Look at the map. Answer the questions about directions in this town.

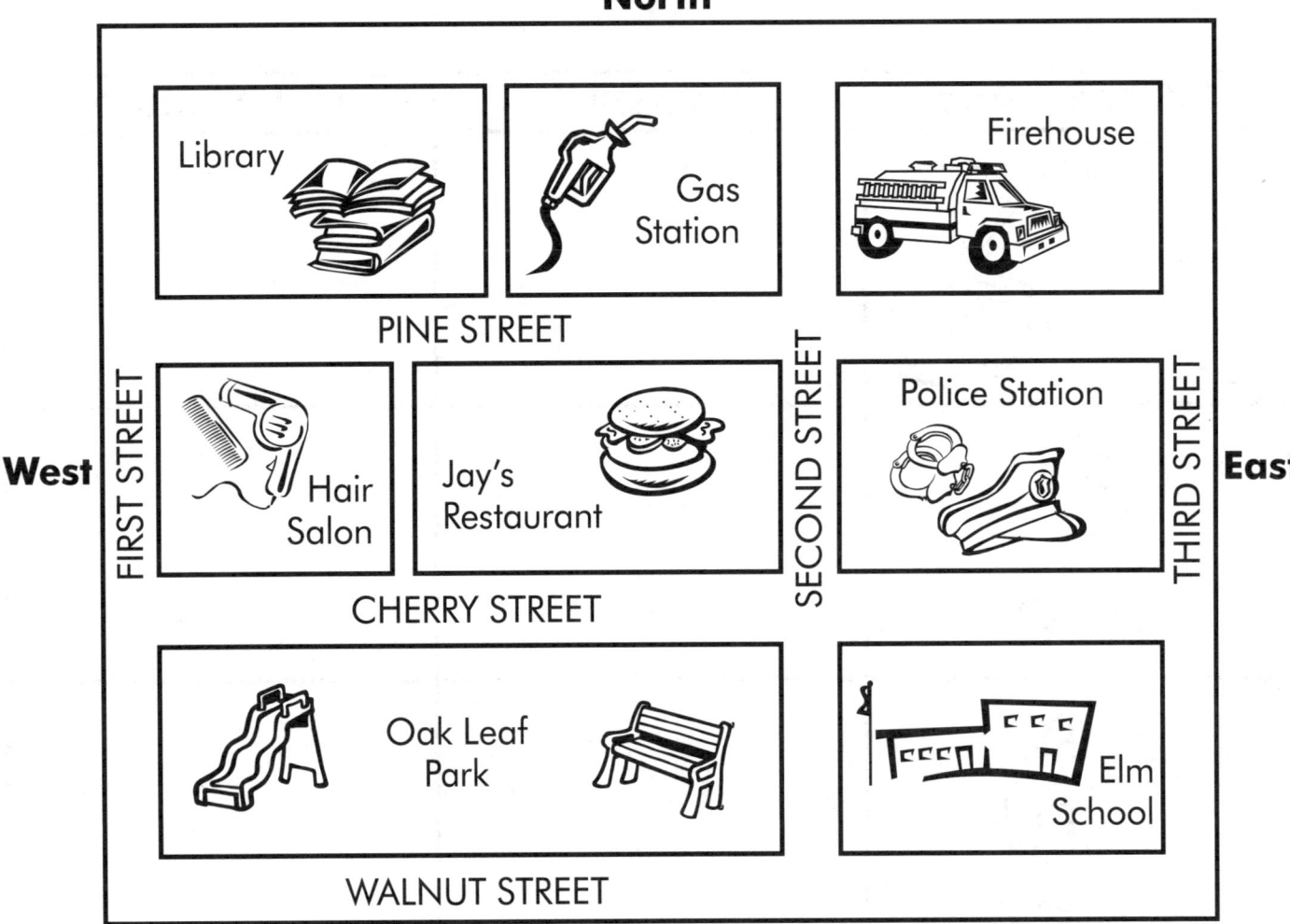

1. Is the Library north or south of the Hair Salon? _____

2. Is Oak Leaf Park east or west of Elm School? _____

3. Is Walnut Street north or south of Cherry Street? _____

4. Is the Police Station east or west of Jay's Restaurant? _____

5. Is First Street east or west of Third Street? _____

Name ______________________ Date ______________________

# This Is My State

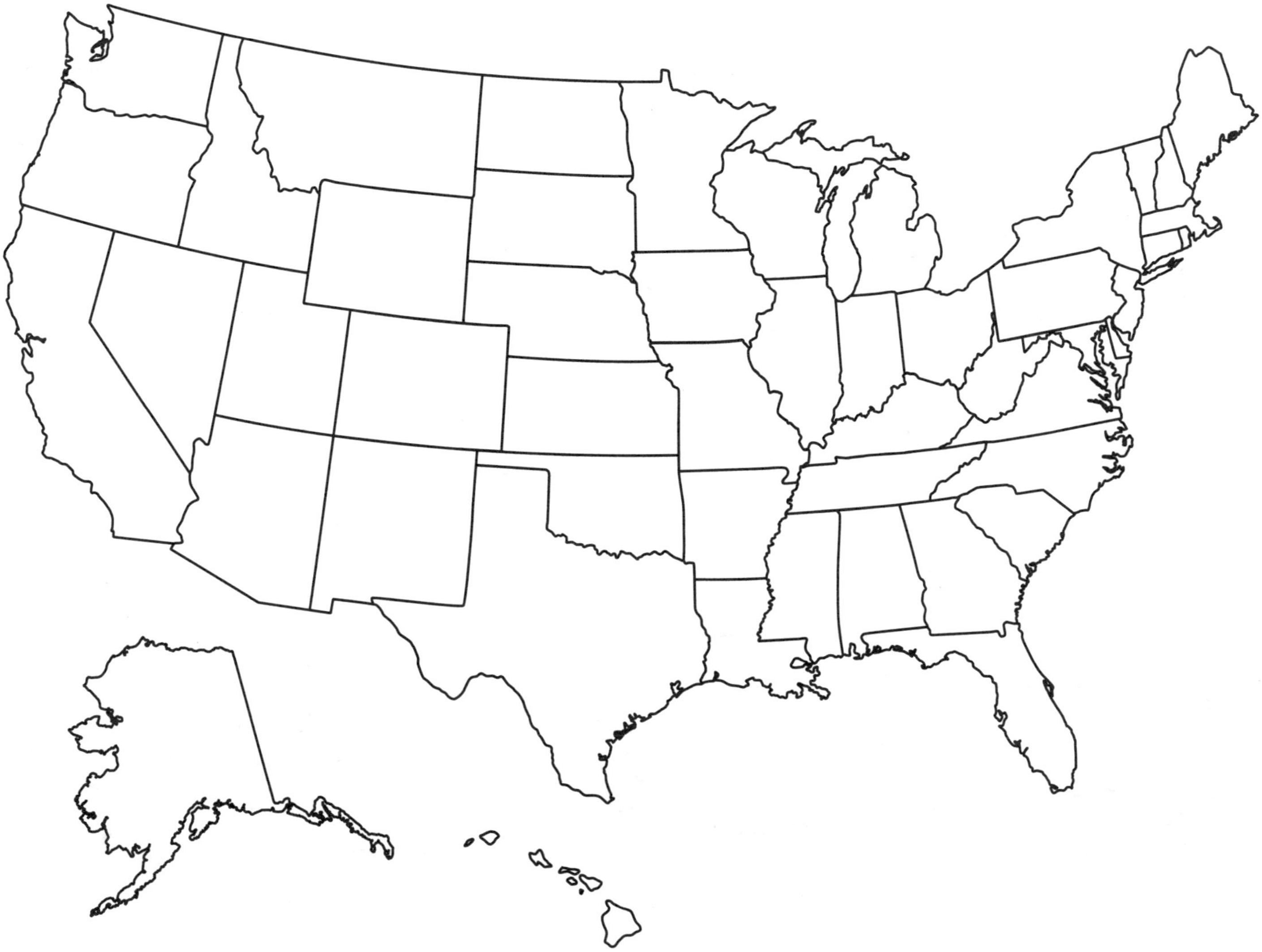

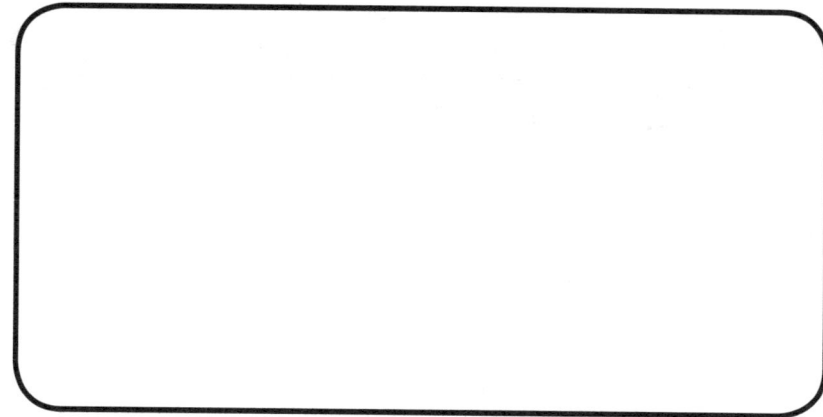

1. Color in your state on the map above.
2. Draw an outline of your state below.

# World Map Jigsaw

Cut out each piece of the puzzle.  Paste them on a piece of paper.
Color your map.

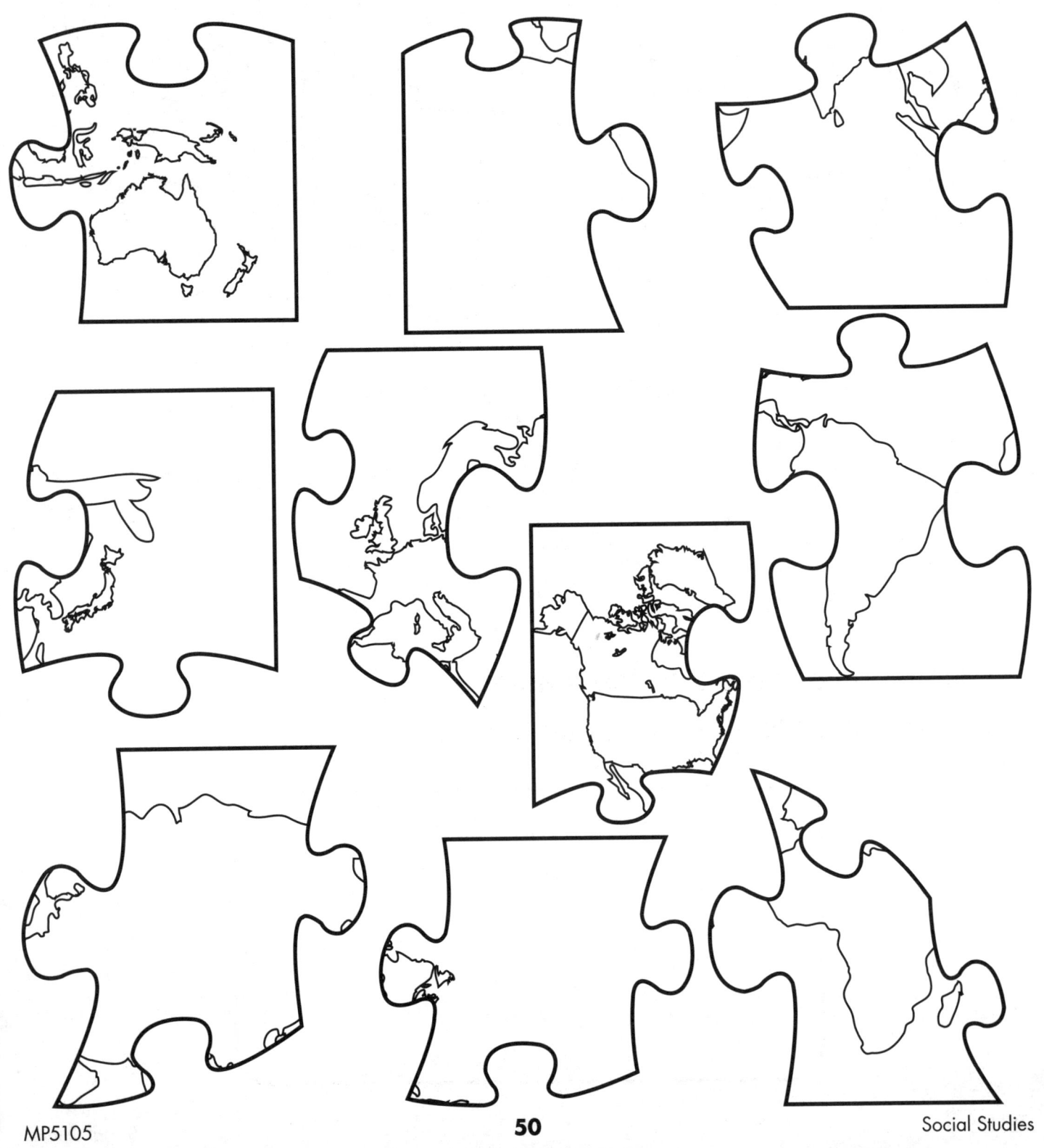

# United States Holidays

Draw a line from the U.S. holiday to its meaning.

1. Martin Luther King, Jr. Day

A. Giving thanks

2. Presidents' Day

B. Honors our nation's workers

3. Independence Day

C. Honors those who fought in wars

4. Memorial Day

D. Honors a man who fought fought for equal rights

5. Labor Day

E. Our nation's birthday

6. Thanksgiving

F. Honors our presidents

Name _____    Date _____

# The United States Flag

Read about the United States flag.  Then answer the questions.

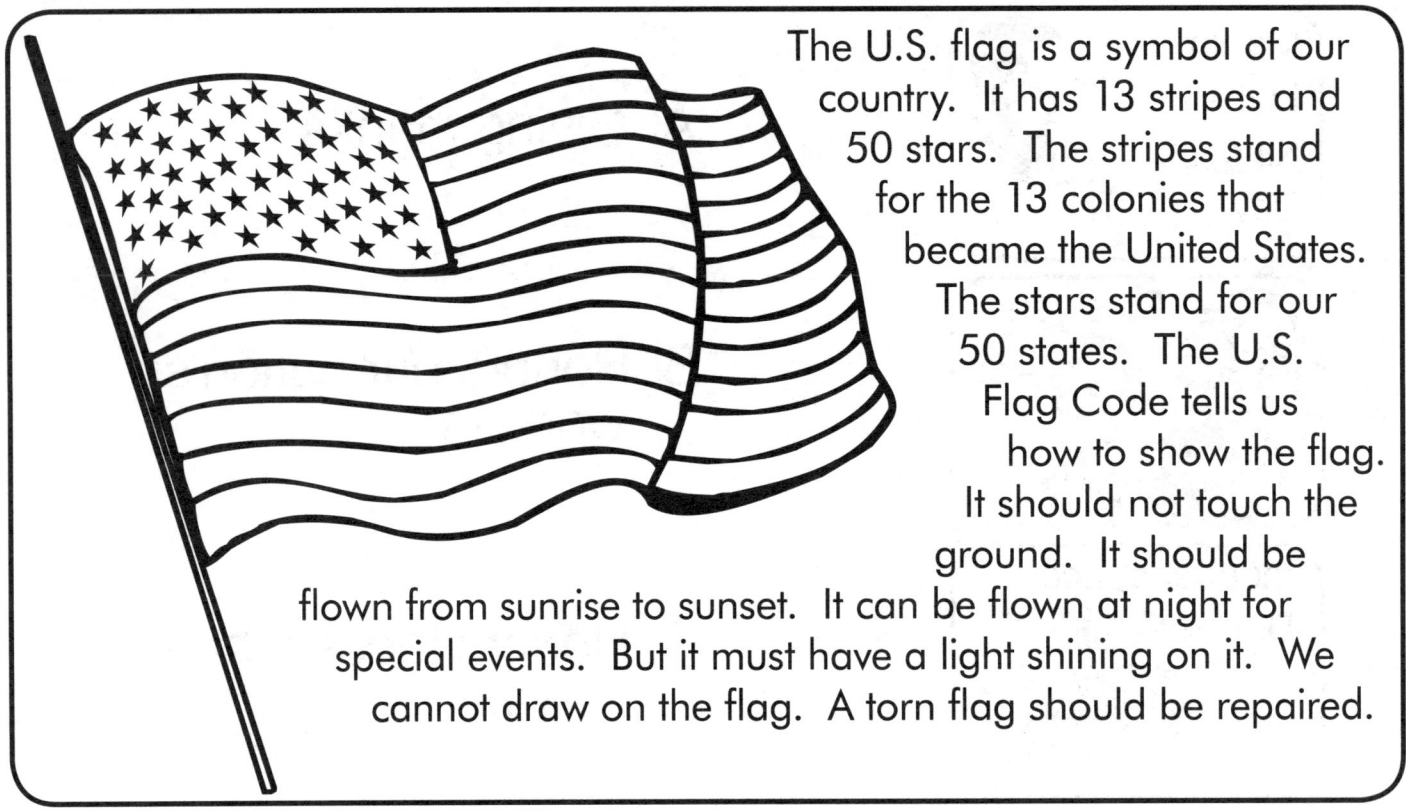

The U.S. flag is a symbol of our country.  It has 13 stripes and 50 stars.  The stripes stand for the 13 colonies that became the United States.  The stars stand for our 50 states.  The U.S. Flag Code tells us how to show the flag.  It should not touch the ground.  It should be flown from sunrise to sunset.  It can be flown at night for special events.  But it must have a light shining on it.  We cannot draw on the flag.  A torn flag should be repaired.

## Circle true or false.

1. The flag has 10 stripes.                              True / False

2. The flag has 50 stars.                                True / False

3. The flag should not touch the ground.                 True / False

4. A flag can be flown at night for special events.      True / False

5. We can draw on the flag.                              True / False

# The Pledge of Allegiance

Fill in the Pledge of Allegiance with words from the list.

| allegiance | pledge | liberty | justice | indivisible |
|---|---|---|---|---|

I _____ _____ to the flag

of the United States of America and to the

republic for which it stands:  one nation under

God, _____ , with

_____ and _____ for all.

**53**

# Symbols of the United States

Color these symbols of the United States.

**54**

# My State Flag

Draw a picture of your state flag.  Tell what the symbols mean.

# Our Elected Leaders

Fill in the names of our elected leaders.

1. Our President is _____ .

2. Our Vice President is _____ .

3. Our state's governor is _____ .

4. Our city's mayor is _____ .

5. What other elected leaders do you know? _____

_____

_____

# The White House

Read about the White House.  Then cut out the strips and put the picture together.

The White House is our president's home.  It has been around for 200 years.  It is in Washington, D.C.  Every president who has lived there has made changes to it.  There are 132 rooms and 6 floors.  If you were one of the president's kids, you could play tennis there or swim in the pool.  You could see movies.  You would meet people from all around the world.  And you would probably have your picture taken a lot!  Would you like to live in the White House?

# American Landmarks Word Search

Here are six American landmarks.

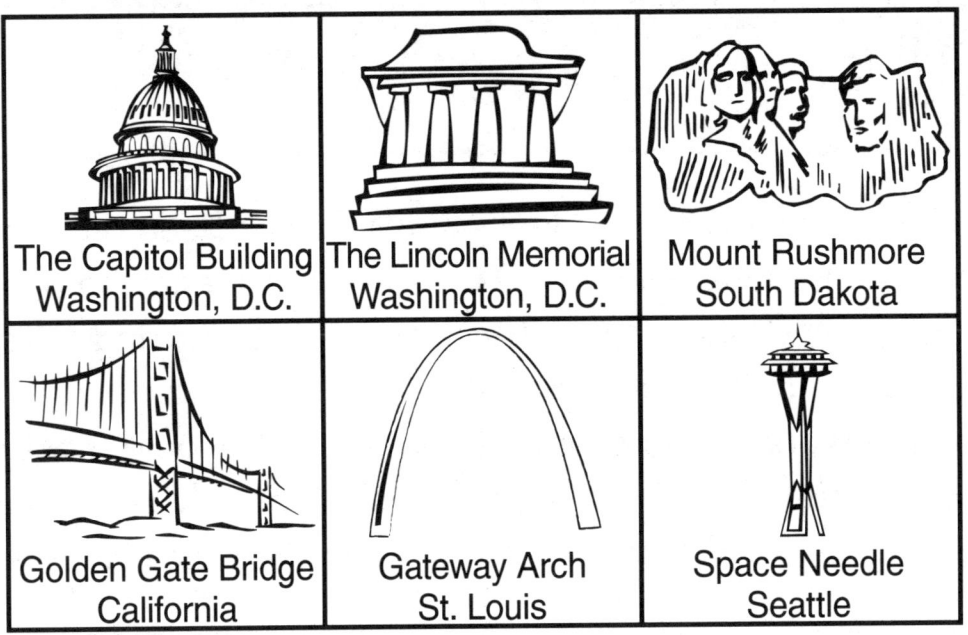

The Capitol Building
Washington, D.C.

The Lincoln Memorial
Washington, D.C.

Mount Rushmore
South Dakota

Golden Gate Bridge
California

Gateway Arch
St. Louis

Space Needle
Seattle

Circle the words in the puzzle below.

| GATEWAY | NEEDLE | RUSHMORE | LINCOLN | SPACE |
|---------|--------|----------|---------|-------|
| ARCH | GOLDEN | CAPITOL | WASHINGTON | BRIDGE |

```
C   F   H   J   X   N   V   C   T   R
W   A   G   A   T   E   W   A   Y   U
A   V   G   R   I   E   O   P   U   S
S   P   A   C   E   D   V   I   U   H
H   B   Q   H   P   L   V   T   L   M
I   X   Z   S   M   E   J   O   L   O
N   P   L   I   N   C   O   L   N   R
G   O   L   D   E   N   X   Z   M   E
T   A   S   Q   U   I   O   V   C   F
O   S   M   P   A   K   X   P   X   H
N   P   S   A   B   R   I   D   G   E
```

# Presidents and Coins

Which presidents' pictures are on U.S. coins?  Cut out each picture on the right.  Paste it on the correct coin on the left.

1. Dime

A. John F. Kennedy

2. Penny

B. George Washington

3. Nickle

C. Franklin D. Roosevelt

4. Quarter

D. Thomas Jefferson

5. Half-dollar

E. Abraham Lincoln

# Famous American Inventors

Here are six American inventors.

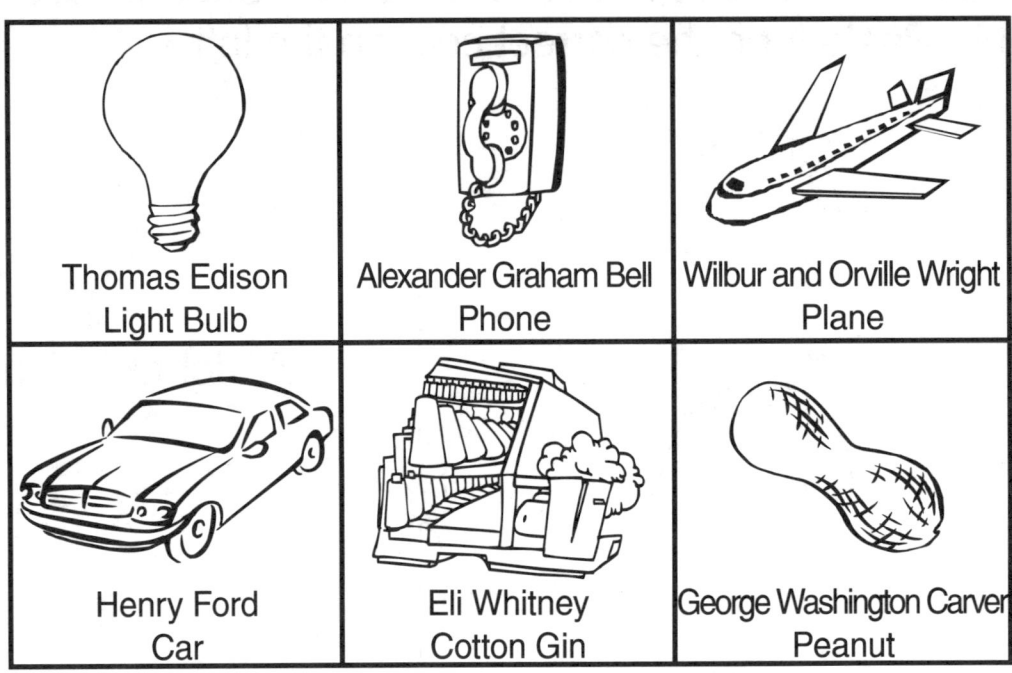

Fill in each sentence with the correct name.

1. I invented the moving assembly line.  My company still makes cars.

   _____

   _ _ _ _ _ _ _ _ _ _

   I am _____ .

2. I invented the cotton gin.  It takes seeds out of cotton.

   _____

   _ _ _ _ _ _ _ _ _ _

   I am _____ .       _____

                                     _ _ _ _ _ _ _ _ _ _

3. I invented the telephone.  I am    _____ .

                                     _____

                                     _ _ _ _ _ _ _ _ _ _

4. I invented the electric light bulb.  I am  _____ .

                                     _____

                                     _ _ _ _ _ _ _ _ _ _

5. I found 300 uses for peanuts.  I am  _____ .

                                     _____

                                     _ _ _ _ _ _ _ _ _ _

6. We flew the world's first airplane.  We are  _____ .

# Goods or Services?

Write whether the person or business provides a **good** or a **service**.

**Goods** are things you buy and use.  They are actual things you can touch.
**Services** are things you pay people to do for you.

_____

_ _ _ _ _ _ _ _ _ _ _ _ _

_____

_ _ _ _ _ _ _ _ _ _ _ _ _

_____

_ _ _ _ _ _ _ _ _ _ _ _ _

_____

_ _ _ _ _ _ _ _ _ _ _ _ _

_____

_ _ _ _ _ _ _ _ _ _ _ _ _

_____

_ _ _ _ _ _ _ _ _ _ _ _ _

_____

_ _ _ _ _ _ _ _ _ _ _ _ _

_____

_ _ _ _ _ _ _ _ _ _ _ _ _

_____

_ _ _ _ _ _ _ _ _ _ _ _ _

# Producers or Consumers?

Write whether the person or business is a **producer** or **consumer**.

> A **producer** makes goods or provides services.
> **Consumers** buy goods and services.

_____

_____

_____

_____

_____

_____

_____

_____

_____

# Proud to Be You and Me!

Cut out the puzzle parts.  Fit them together.  Glue them onto a separate page.  Color your picture!

# Science

These Physical Science, Life Science, and Earth Science activities heighten students' awareness of the world around them, including materials that compose our earth and our atmosphere and the needs of plants and animals. Students also strengthen their lifelong process of observing, asking questions about, and recording the events of their environment. Encourage your students to use their senses when describing plants, animals, weather, and seasonal changes. Above all, with every activity, continue to foster respect for the environment and for the interdependent web of life of which we are all a part.

| Activity Title | Page | Content Standard and Skills Reinforced | EXTRA! Extension Activities |
|---|---|---|---|
| Solid, Liquid, or Gas? | 67 | The three forms of matter | Review the concept of matter: gas is invisible and can easily change shape, liquids are visible and take the shape of whatever they are put in, and solids keep their shape. Ask students to point out some matter that may change shape (water may convert to ice and vice versa due to temperature changes). Point out various items in the classroom, and ask whether they are solid, liquid, or gas. Have students write these additional items where they belong on the graphic organizer. |
| What Does a Magnet Attract? | 68 | Properties of a magnet | Do this activity as a group. Hold several metal and nonmetal objects to a magnet, and have students fill in the circles with those objects that the magnet attracts. Answers include paper clips, thumb tacks, keys, pins, nails, screws, the pocket clips on pens, and other magnets. |
| The Parts of a Plant | 69 | Identifying basic parts of a plant | Review the basic plant parts and the purpose of each: leaves (photosynthesis), stem (support plant, provides a place for the plant to keep its leaves, fruits, and flowers), roots (absorb water and nutrients and anchor the plant in the ground), flower (carries/releases seeds). Point out these various parts on plants you have in your classroom. |
| Leaf Rubbing | 70 | Identifying the parts of a leaf | Show students how to do a leaf rubbing. Help each of them find one leaf and have them do a rubbing with crayon or pencil. Then work together with them to identify the simple parts of the leaf, no matter what kind of leaf it is. Discuss the purpose of leaves in making food from sunlight. |
| What a Plant Needs | 71 | Identifying the basic needs of a plant | Discuss the basic concept of survival. Review what a plant needs to survive. Discuss the fact that different plants have different temperature, light, and nutrient needs. What plants and crops, for example, grow in your area or cannot grow in your area because of their requirements for survival? |
| How Seeds Travel | 72 | Seed dispersal | Discuss the various ways that seeds are dispersed—wind; water; getting stuck to fur, clothes, mud on shoes, etc. Ask if students have ever planted a garden and then found that something appeared they didn't plant. Have them speculate about how the "volunteer" plant got there. Have students think of other seeds that would travel by wind, animals, people, or water. |
| What Plants Give Us Word Scramble | 73 | What plants give us for survival and enjoyment | Discuss the additional things that we get from plants: beauty for our homes, yards, and communities; the oxygen we breathe; medicines; prevention of soil erosion; other products derived from plants, such as inks and dyes, etc. |
| Animal Homes | 74 | Different animals inhabit different environments | Review students' answers for each type of animal home and write them on the board. Ask, "Why does this animal need this type of home?" Discuss animals' shelter needs. Example: "Why would a bear live in a cave instead of a stable?" |
| What Does It Eat? | 75 | Animal diets | Discuss how animals are categorized according to their diets: plants and meat (omnivore), meat (carnivore), plants (herbivore), and insects (insectivore). Wolves eat deer and other animals they catch in the wild; frogs eat insects; giraffes eat leaves, shrubs, vines, and herbs; chimpanzees eat fruit, nuts, berries, insects, and small mammals; and deer eat leaves, fruit, acorns, vines, and grasses. Ask students to name other animals and what they eat, including domestic animals. |

| | | | |
|---|---|---|---|
| Animals Get Ready for Winter | 76 | How animals prepare for winter by migrating, adaptation, storing, or hibernating | Discuss how people get ready for winter in cold-weather climates (clothing, preparing the house, preparing the car). Then discuss that animals, too, must prepare for the winter season. Review migration, adaptation, storing, and hibernating. Students are fascinated with the concept of hibernation. Ask, "Which animals, in addition to some bears, go dormant during winter?" (Answers include some bats, butterflies, snakes, squirrels, wasps, and turtles.) |
| Fur, Feathers, or Scales? | 77 | Categorizing | After you review the activity, have students find other examples of animals that have fur, feathers, or scales. Talk about how these animal coverings help the animals cope with their environments. |
| Now You See It! Now You Don't! | 78 | •Animal camouflage and mimicry •Shape recognition | Review the meaning of the terms camouflage and mimicry. Discuss the fact that camouflage and mimicry help animals survive in their environment. What local animals, insects, or birds are known for their camouflage or mimicry ability? |
| Frog Life Cycle | 79 | Frog life cycle | Do this same activity for butterflies, birds, and other animals in an animal life cycle unit. |
| Who Am I? | 80 | •Scientists make a contribution to society •Reading a narrative passage •Wildlife protection | If possible, show some additional pictures of Jane Goodall. Show The Jane Goodall Institute website (www.janegoodall.org) and discuss her Roots & Shoots program for youth, or show one of the many TV programs featuring Goodall, such as Nova. |
| My Favorite Animal | 81 | Fostering appreciation and respect for animals | Encourage students to draw birds, insects, reptiles, or mammals. Have each student tell why his or her chosen animal is a favorite. Ask students what they could do to ensure that these animals are protected for the future. Display their finished pictures on a bulletin board labeled "Our Favorite Animals." |
| Color the Rainbow | 82 | Rainbows are refracted and reflect light rays | Make sure that students have the rainbow colors in the correct order: red (at the top edge), orange, yellow, green, blue, indigo, violet. Review the fact that the light rays are refracted and reflected by the raindrops. Ask students if they have heard stories about rainbows (such as a pot of gold at the end of the rainbow). Why do people think of rainbows as magical? |
| What's the Temperature? | 83 | Reading a thermometer | Review how the mercury on a thermometer moves as the temperature changes. Show students how to color in the thermometers on the activity sheets. After reviewing the activity sheet, give students several sample situations and ask them what the temperature might be on that particular day—for example, a day at the beach, a day to make a snowman, a day to plant flowers, or a day to rake falling leaves. |
| What Does Weather Mean? | 84 | The elements of weather | Ask, "What is the weather today?" Then review each element on the activity, asking, for example, what the temperature is, whether it's sunny or cloudy, rainy, foggy, etc. |
| Weather Words | 85 | Weather terminology | You may wish to do this activity with the whole class. Discuss students' experiences with dew, fog, frost, and smog. (Students in urban areas will likely be more familiar with smog. Your local weather forecasters may even give smog alerts. If so, discuss what people can do to stay healthy on smog alert days.) You may wish to have students draw a picture incorporating one or two of the words and display them on a bulletin board labeled "Weather Words." |
| Weather Report | 86 | •Observing and describing the weather •Summarizing •Printing legibly | You may want to do this activity together as a class. Allow students to write in the boxes or draw pictures of the weather today. Then work with them to summarize the information by giving an example: "Today it is 68 degrees. It is cloudy. It is raining and windy." |
| This Week's Weather | 87 | •Recording observations on a bar graph •Seasonal temperatures tend to be predictable | Distribute this activity on a Monday and review it on a Friday or the following Monday. Work with students to write the temperature each day at lunchtime on this sheet. Then show them how to record the information on the bar graph. What does this bar graph allow us to see? (Seasonal temperatures tend to be predictable.) |
| Types of Clouds | 88 | Types of clouds | Review that clouds perform several functions, including providing rain and snow. Have students generate sentences about each type of cloud, using the terms from the activity. |

| | | | |
|---|---|---|---|
| Picture in a Cloud | 89 | •Cloud identification<br>•Identifying objects in the sky<br>•Shape recognition | Cloud-watching is fun! You may do this activity with the class by having them look out the window or go outside on a fairly cloudy day. Have students share their pictures and tell what they think their clouds looked like. Did any students draw the same image without conferring with each other? Display the pictures on a bulletin board labeled "Cloud Pictures." |
| Watch Out for Bad Weather | 90 | •Describing types of bad weather<br>•Printing legibly | Have students share their pictures. Review what creates each of these types of weather. Some students may not have experienced all of these types of weather. Encourage students to share their experiences and how they kept safe. |
| Sensing the Season | 91 | Using the senses to gather and interpret information about the environment | Use this activity for any season. Encourage all students to participate in the discussion, including students who are physically challenged. Focus on interpretation of the information. Example: "You are seeing leaves fall from the trees. Why is this happening?" |
| Sort These Recyclables | 92 | •The importance of caring for the environment by recycling<br>•Categorizing recyclables | Discuss why recycling is good for the environment and helps conserve resources. Also discuss the fact that cans and bottles should be rinsed before they're put in the recycle bin. Some communities require you to separate glass by color, paper by type of paper, etc. Also talk about articles that cannot be recycled at home but can be recycled at a recycling center, such as car batteries, paint, and motor oil. Post the address/phone number of your county recycling center. |
| Stop the Air Pollution Now! | 93 | Major causes of air pollution and how to prevent them | Do this activity with students. Review the meaning of pollution. Talk about the effects that air pollution has on our lungs and overall health and quality of life. Then review these three key ways students can prevent air pollution: composting instead of burning trash and leaves; riding a bike instead of riding in an automobile (about half of air pollution comes from vehicle emissions); planting trees. |
| I Can Make a Difference! | 94 | •Community responsibility<br>•Environmental awareness | Review these practical ways students can help protect our environment. Post them on a bulletin board and label the exhibit "I Can Make a Difference!" |

# Solid, Liquid, or Gas?

All matter in the world is a solid, liquid, or gas.  Write each word where it belongs.

| helium | seashell | hydrogen |
| pencil | water | oxygen |
| juice | leaf | milk |

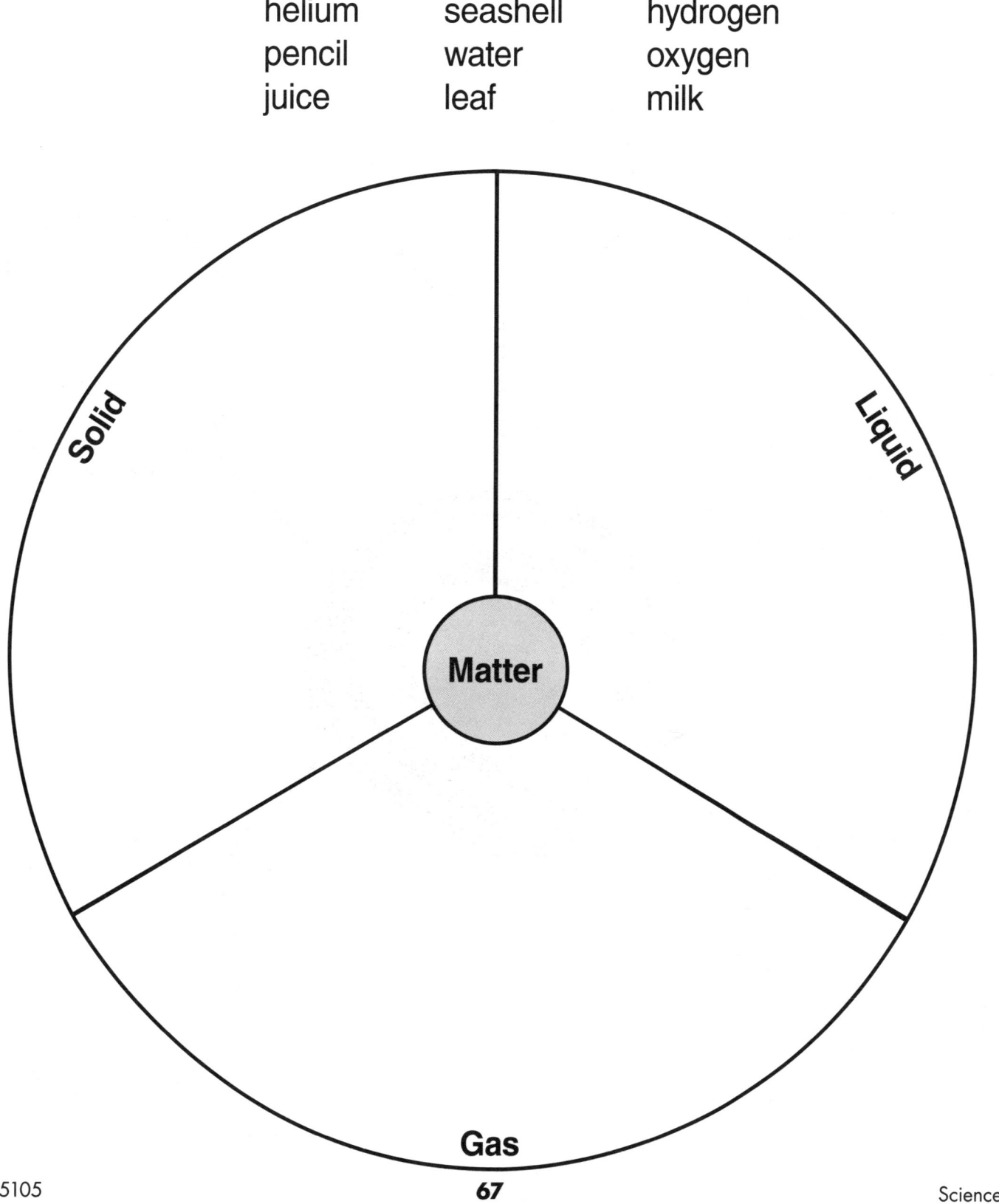

# What Does a Magnet Attract?

Draw something in each circle that a magnet attracts.

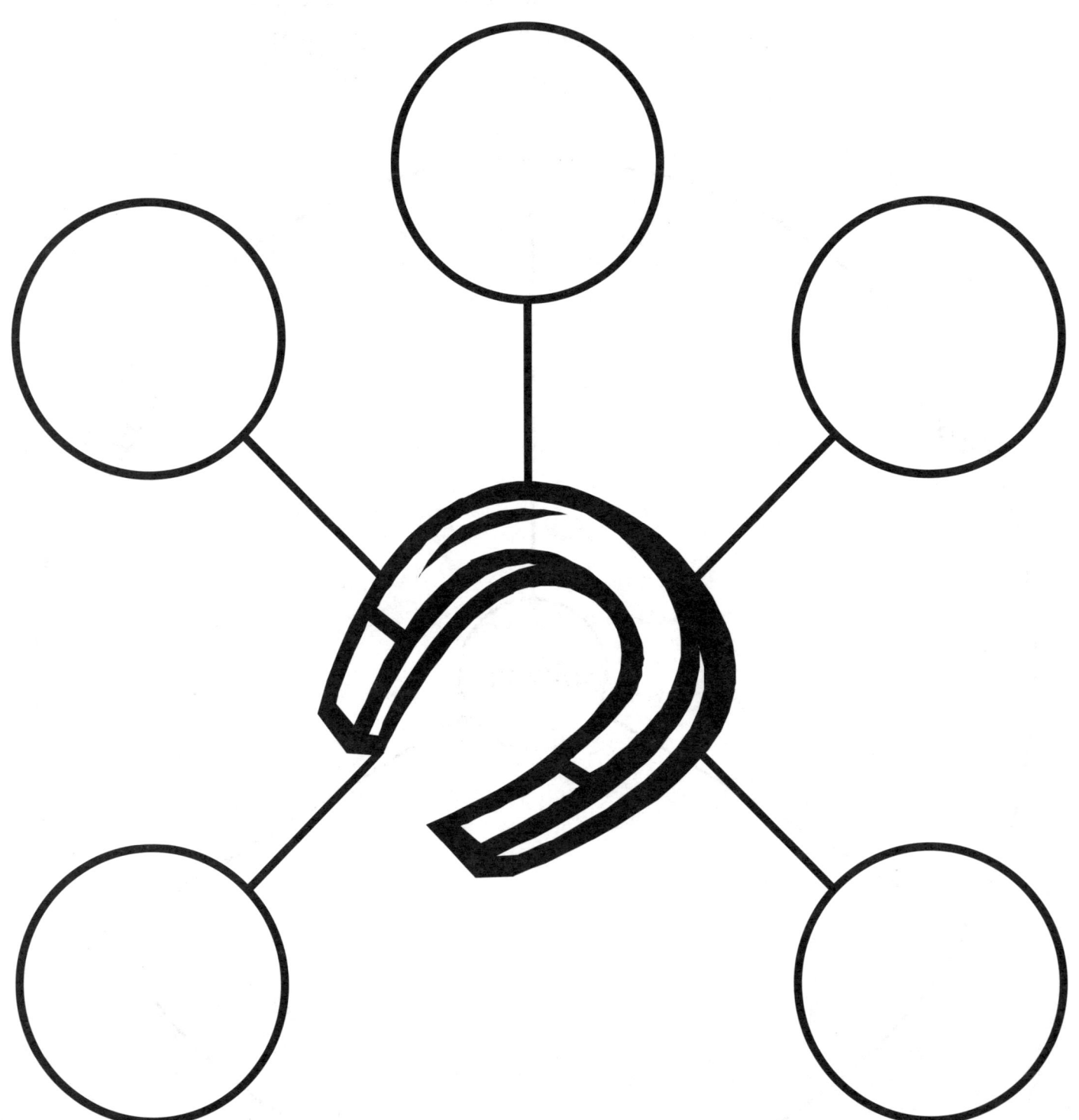

# The Parts of a Plant

Write the plant part where it belongs.  Color the plant.

| leaf | flower | stem | root | seed |
|------|--------|------|------|------|

# Leaf Rubbing

Find a leaf, and do a rubbing of it.  Then label each part of the leaf.

| blade | midrib | vein | petiole |

**70**

# What a Plant Needs

Plants need four things to grow.  Cut out each picture at the bottom.
Paste it in the correct box.

**SOIL**

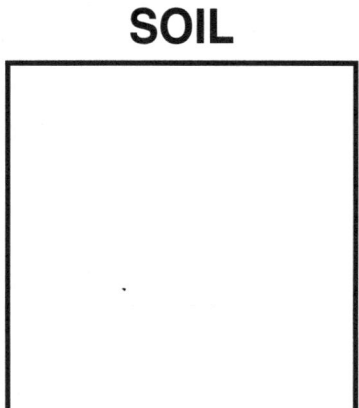

Gives water and food to the roots

**AIR**

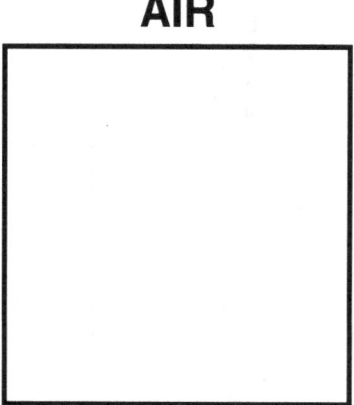

Helps plants make their food

**WATER**

Helps plants make their food

**LIGHT**

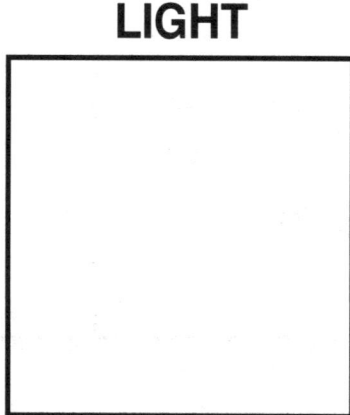

Plants turn it into food

Name _____ Date _____

# How Seeds Travel

Cut out the pictures.  Paste them in the row that tells how the seeds travel.

| | |
|---|---|
| Seeds carried by **WIND** | |
| Seeds carried by **ANIMALS OR PEOPLE** | |
| Seeds carried by **WATER** | |

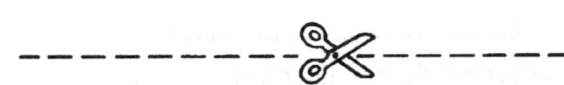

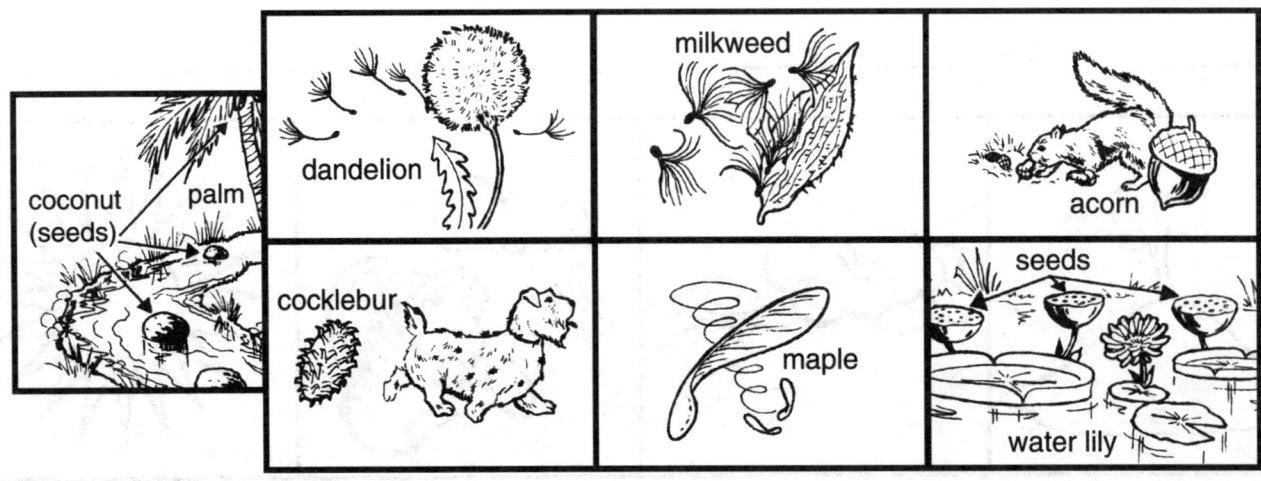

# What Plants Give Us

People and animals need plants!  Unscramble the letters that tell some things we get from plants.

OODF  _____

TSNE  _____

DESHA  _____

EPRO  _____

TTCOON  _____

PAOS  _____

# Animal Homes

Write the name of a **bird**, **animal**, or **insect** that might live in each of these homes.

_____

- - - - - - - - - - - - -

_____

_____

- - - - - - - - - - - - -

_____

_____

- - - - - - - - - - - - -

_____

_____

- - - - - - - - - - - - -

_____

_____

- - - - - - - - - - - - -

_____

_____

- - - - - - - - - - - - -

_____

_____

- - - - - - - - - - - - -

_____

_____

- - - - - - - - - - - - -

_____

_____

- - - - - - - - - - - - -

_____

# What Does It Eat?

Connect the dots to see what each animal eats!

1.  wolf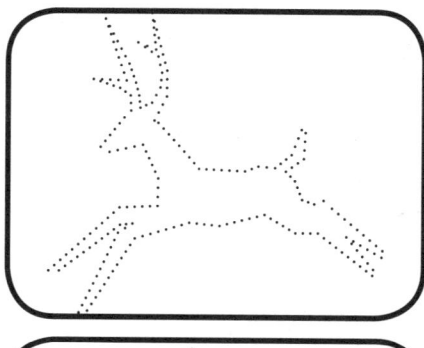

2.  frog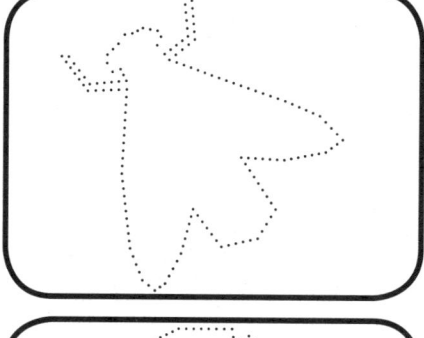

3.  giraffe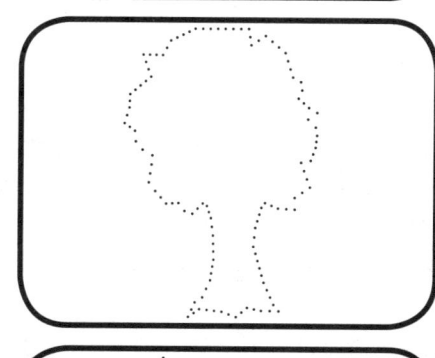

4.  chimpanzee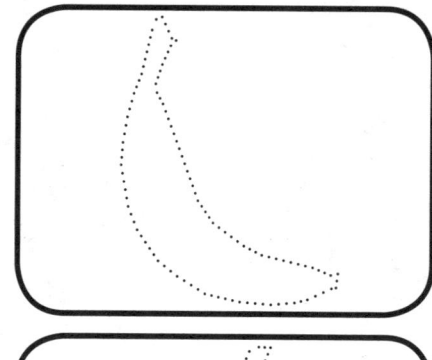

5.  deer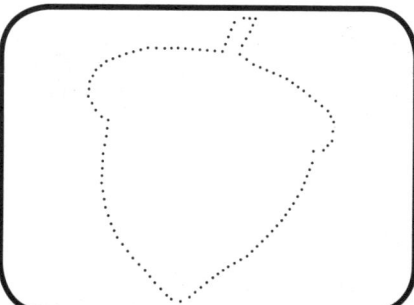

# Animals Get Ready for Winter

Write the word that shows what each animal is doing to prepare for winter.

| storing | hibernating | migrating | adapting |

1. _____

2. _____

3. _____

4. _____

# Fur, Feathers, or Scales?

Write whether each animal has **fur**, **feathers**, or **scales**.

_____

_____

_____

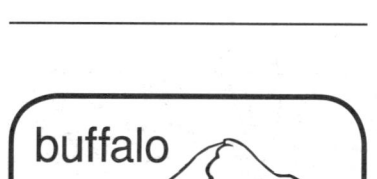

_____

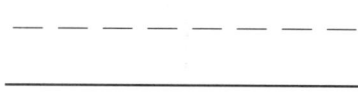

_____

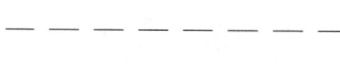

_____

_____

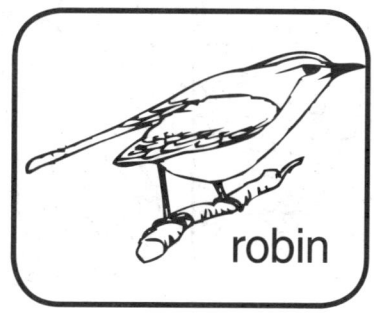

_____

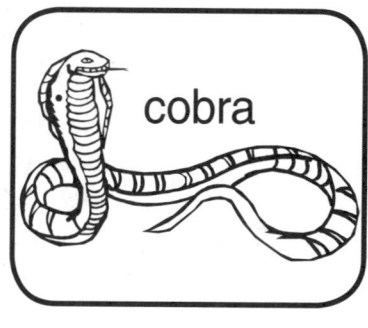

_____

# Now You See It!  Now You Don't!

Some animals blend in with their environments.  Some can change their color.  Color the animal in each picture.  Look hard!

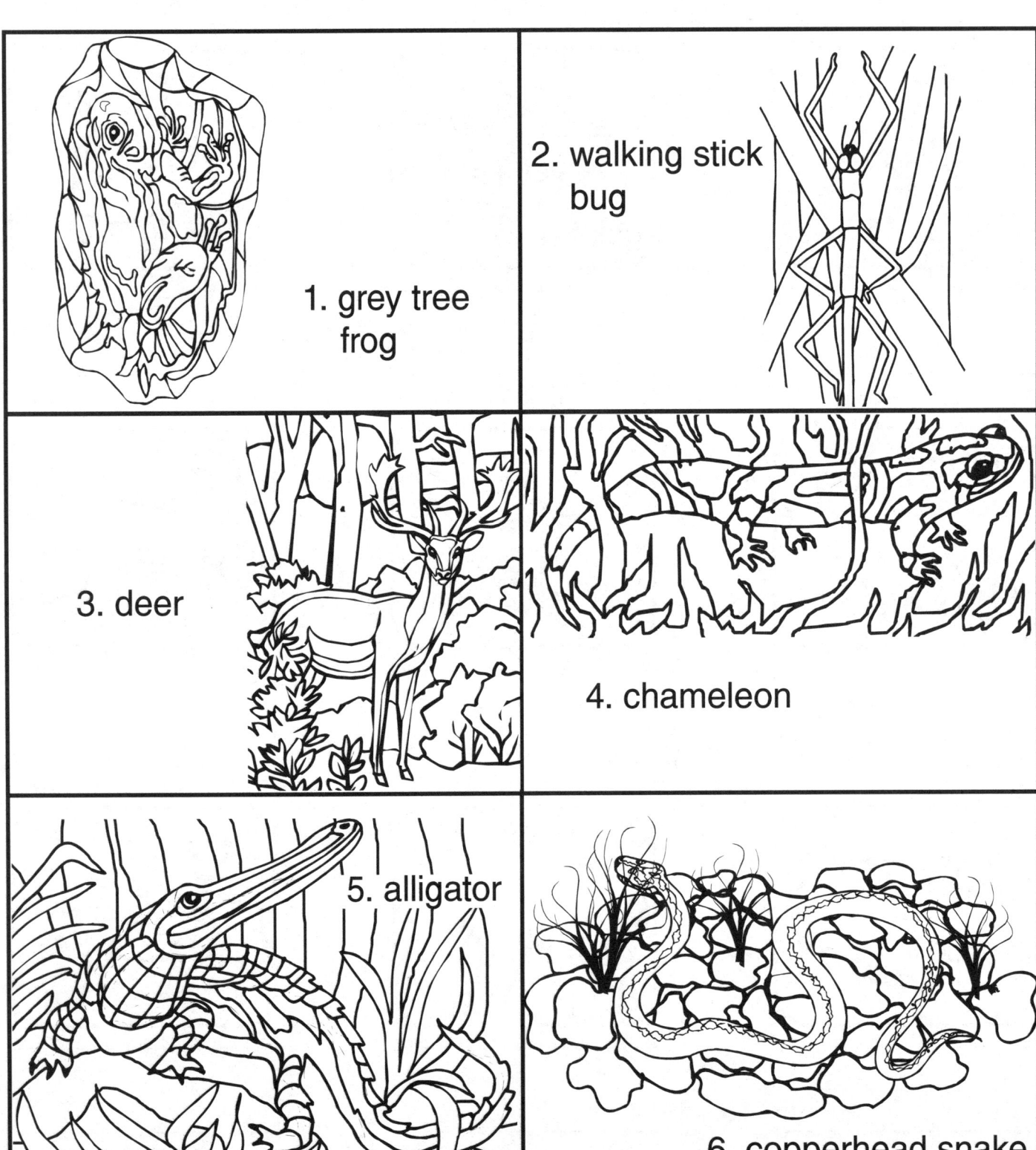

1. grey tree frog

2. walking stick bug

3. deer

4. chameleon

5. alligator

6. copperhead snake

Name _____  Date _____

# Frog Life Cycle

Below are pictures of the frog as it changes and grows.  Cut them out and paste them in order.

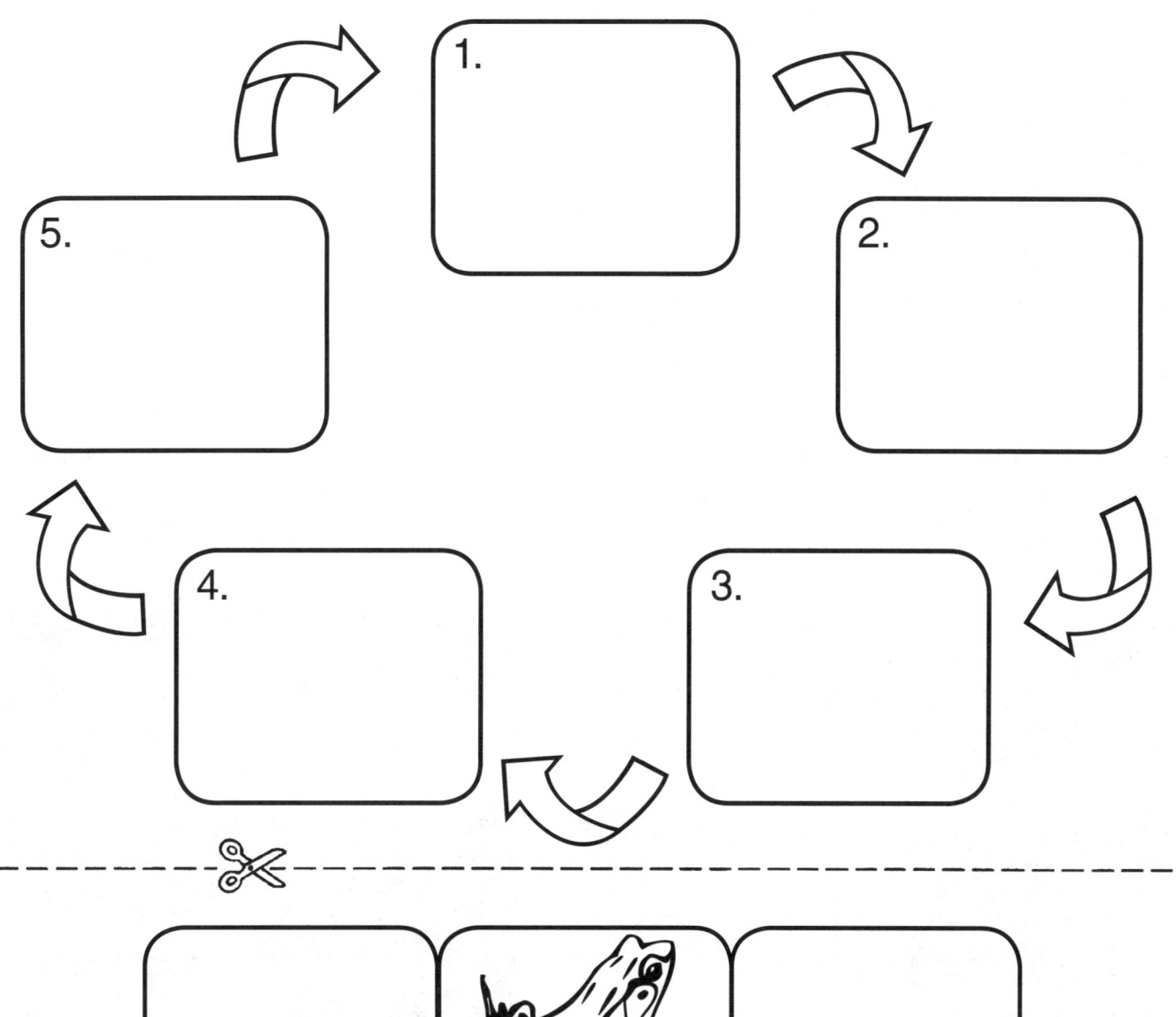

# Who Am I?

Read the story.  Then cut out the puzzle pieces and put them together.  Who is the story about?

I was born in England.  When I was little, my father gave me a stuffed chimpanzee.  I loved that chimpanzee!  After that, I wanted to work with animals.  I have worked with chimpanzees my whole life.  I found out that they make tools from twigs.  I also found out that they live in families.  I write books.  I make movies.  I speak all over the world for animal rights.
**Who am I?**

_____

- - - - - - - - - - - - - - - - - - - - - - - -

_____

✂ - - - - - - - - - - - - - - - - - - - - - - - - - - - -

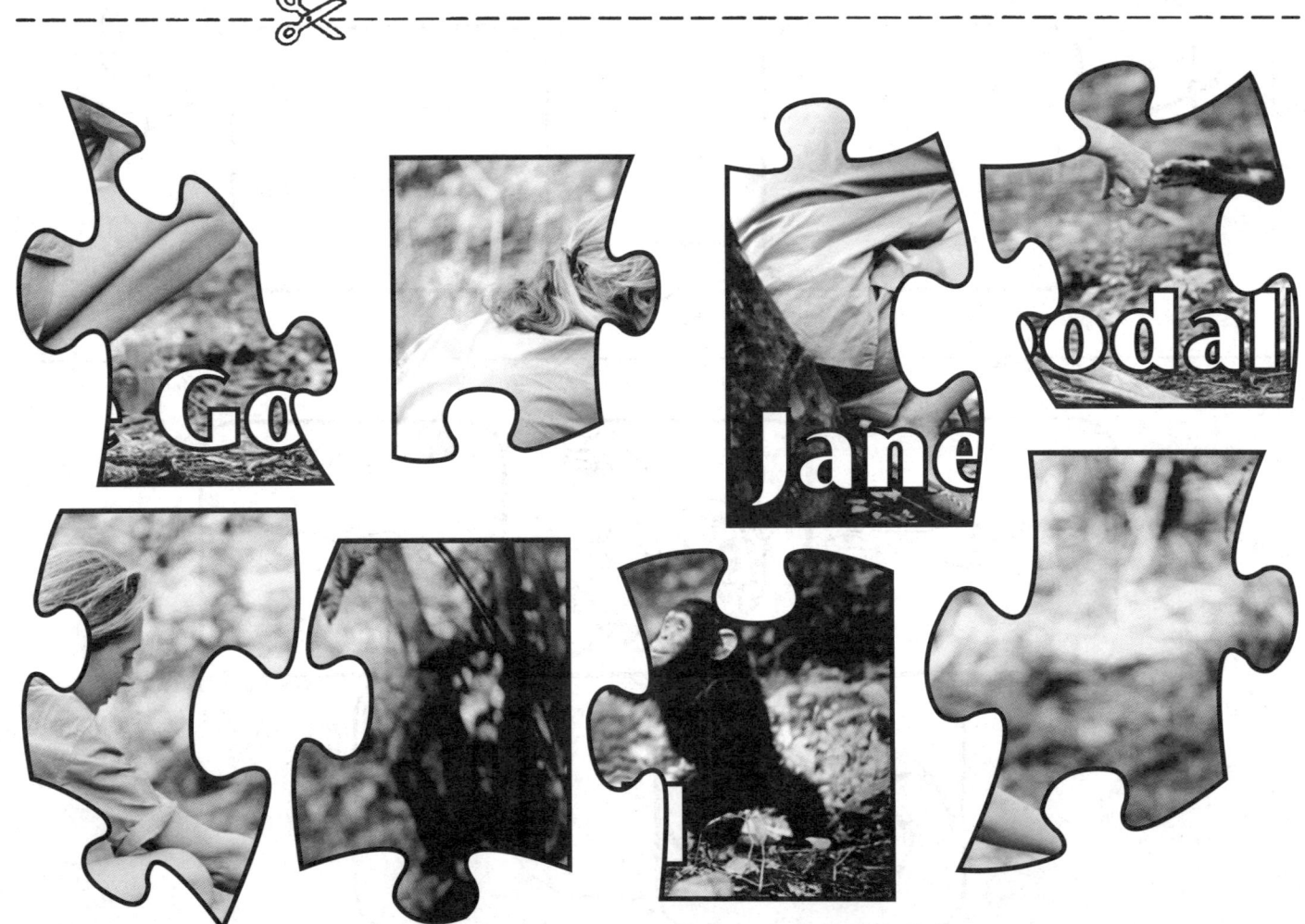

# My Favorite Animal

Draw a picture of your favorite animal.  Tell why you like this animal.

I like this animal because

_____

- - - - - - - - - - - - - - - - - - - - - - - -

_____

_____

- - - - - - - - - - - - - - - - - - - - - - - -

_____

Name _____  Date _____

# Color the Rainbow

You need sunlight and water in the air to have a rainbow.  Color a rainbow in this picture.  Put in the sun and some drops of rain. Make sure you put the colors in the right order!

# What's the Temperature?

Color in each thermometer to show the temperature.

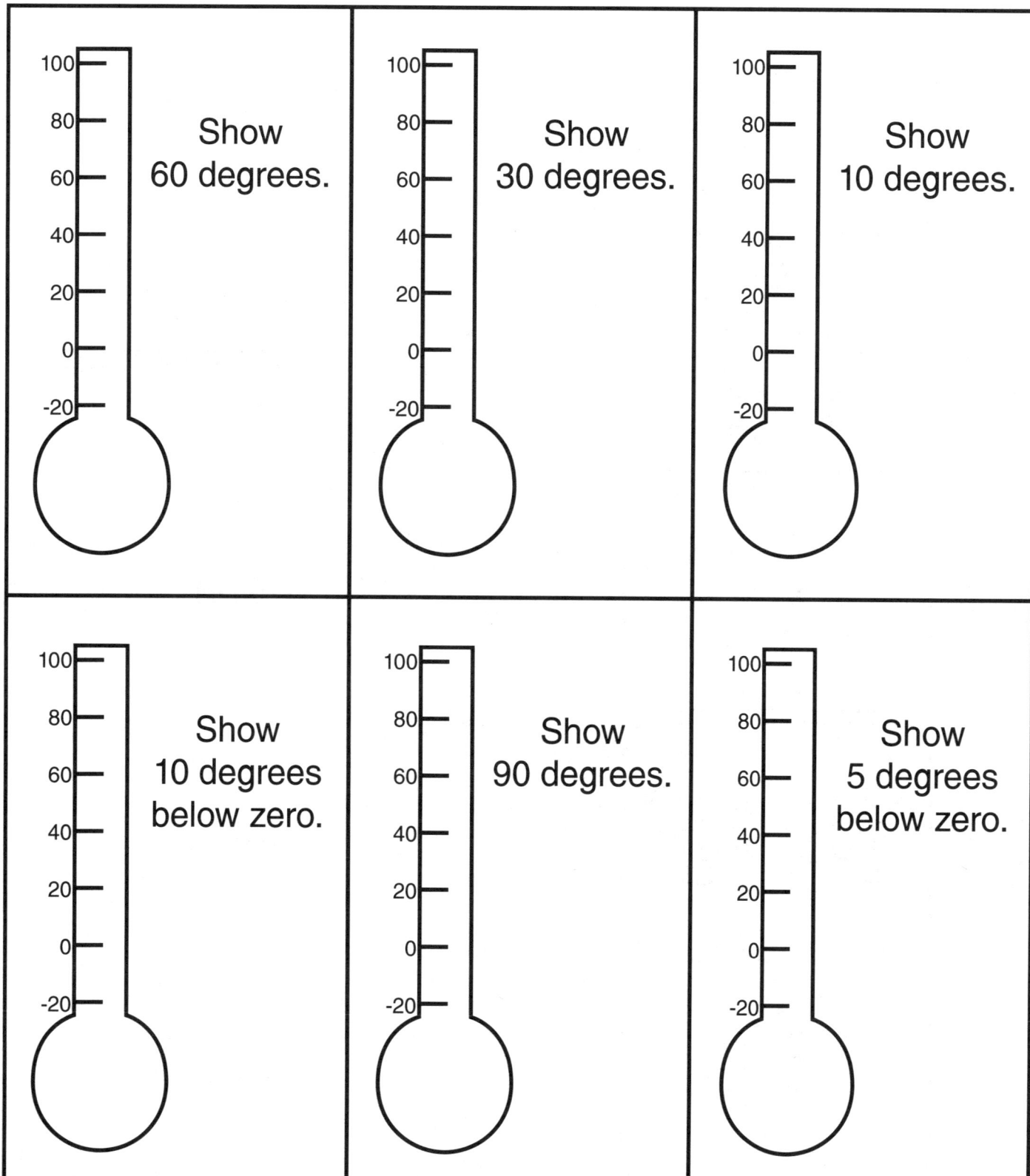

Show
60 degrees.

Show
30 degrees.

Show
10 degrees.

Show
10 degrees
below zero.

Show
90 degrees.

Show
5 degrees
below zero.

# What Does Weather Mean?

Draw a line from the symbols to the words they represent. All of these together make up the weather.

1.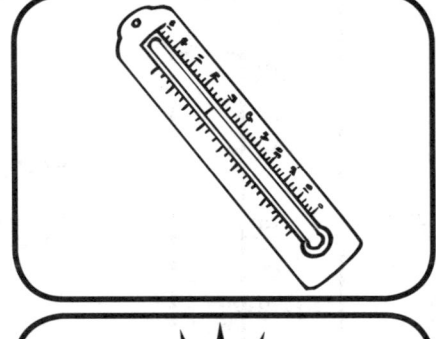

              A. visibility

2.

              B. temperature

3.

              C. wind

4.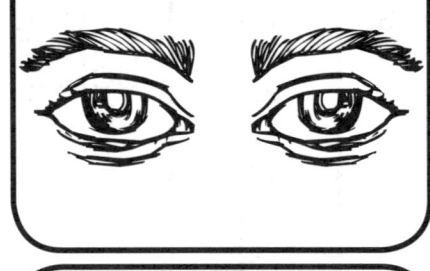

              D. rain

5.

              E. sunshine

# Weather Words

Write the correct weather word into each sentence.

| | | | | |
|---|---|---|---|---|
| air | breeze | dew | freeze | humidity |
| barometer | clouds | fog | frost | smog |

1. A _____ is a gentle wind.

2. _____ is the gases that form the Earth's atmosphere.

3. _____ is water drops you usually see in the morning.

4. A _____ measures air pressure.

5. A _____ happens when the temperature is 32 degrees or below.

6. _____ is white ice crystals.

7. _____ is air pollution you can see.

8. _____ is water vapor or wetness in the air.

9. _____ are masses of water or ice crystals in the air.

10. _____ is a cloud on the ground that makes it hard to see.

# Weather Report

What is the weather today?  Answer the questions.  Then write sentences that give a weather report.

1. 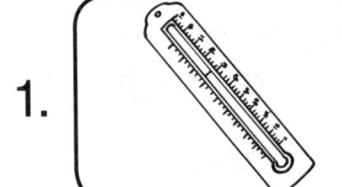 What is the temperature? _____

2.  Is it sunny or cloudy? _____

3.  Is it raining? _____

4.  Is it windy? _____

5.  Is it misty, foggy, or clear? _____

Write a few sentences about the weather today.

_____

_____

_____

_____

Name _____  Date _____

# This Week's Weather

Write the temperature at lunchtime each day this week.  Then color the graph to show how the temperature changed.

| MONDAY | TUESDAY | WEDNESDAY | THURSDAY | FRIDAY |
|---|---|---|---|---|
| Temperature: ____ | Temperature: ____ | Temperature: ____ | Temperature: ____ | Temperature: ____ |

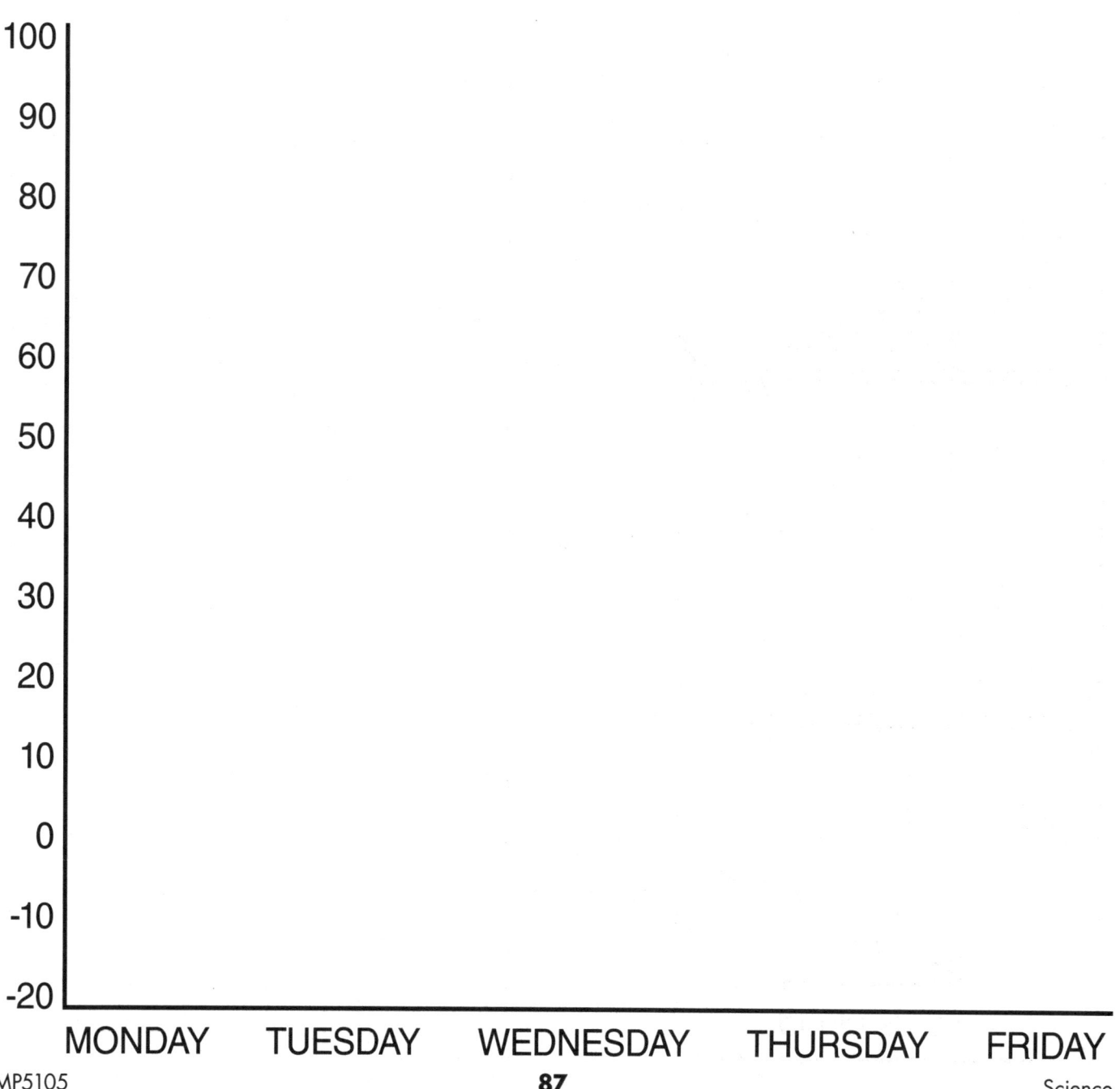

MONDAY    TUESDAY    WEDNESDAY    THURSDAY    FRIDAY

# Types of Clouds

We see three types of clouds in the sky.  We describe them by how they look.  Write each word or phrase next to the cloud it describes.

| | |
|---|---|
| thin | look like flat sheets |
| gray like fog | wispy |
| white and puffy | flat bases and lumpy tops |

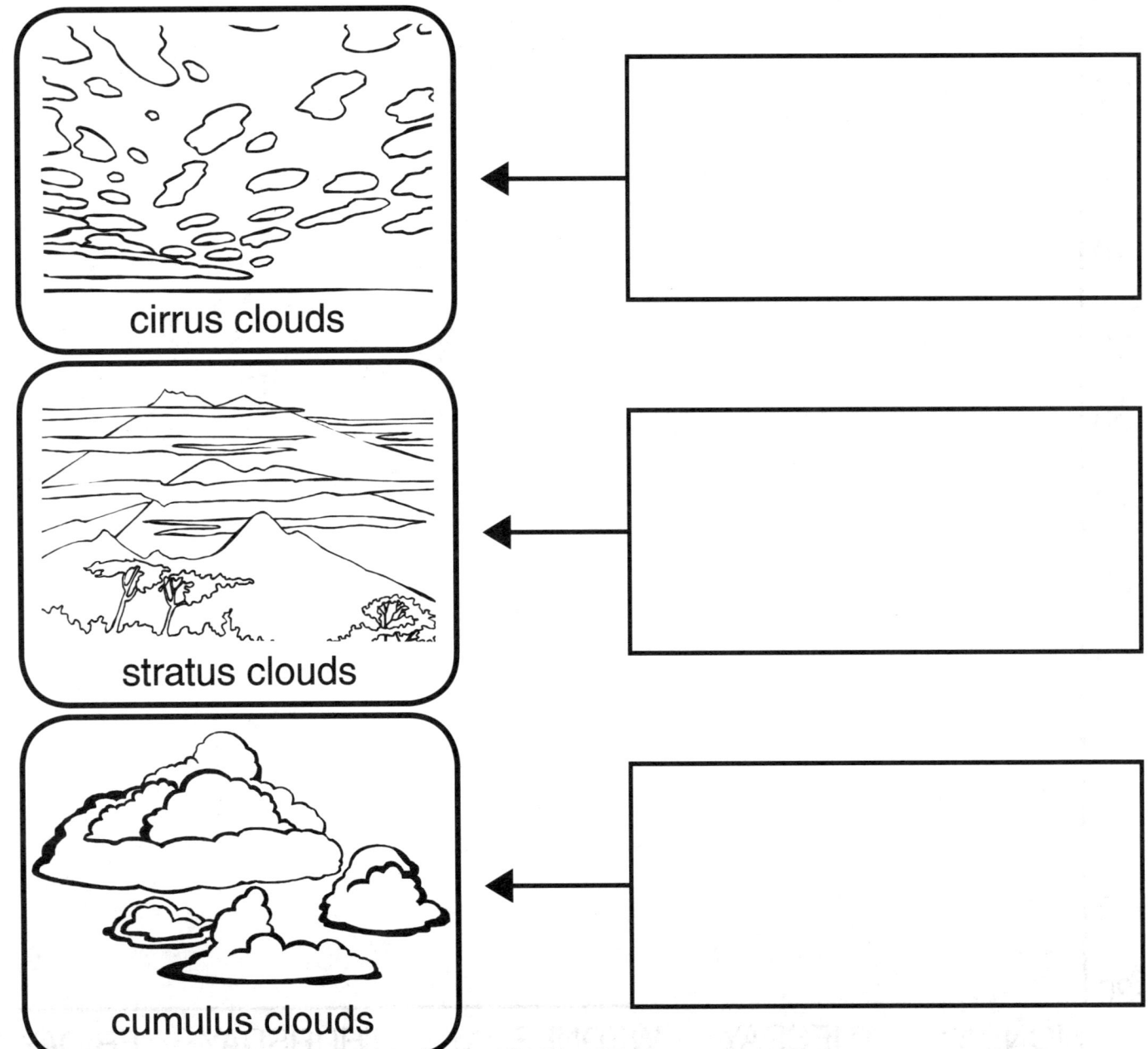

cirrus clouds

stratus clouds

cumulus clouds

# Picture in a Cloud

Have you ever thought a cloud looked like a person, animal, or thing?
Look up at the clouds.  Draw one that looks like a person, animal, or
thing.  Write what you think it looks like.

This cloud looks like

_____

_ _ _ _ _ _ _ _ _ _ _ _ _ _ _ _ _ _ _ _ _ _ _ _ _

_____

# Watch Out for Bad Weather

Choose one of these types of bad weather.  Draw a picture of it.
Then write a sentence about it.

| blizzard | hailstorm | hurricane | thunderstorm | tornado |

_____

- - - - - - - - - - - - - - - - - - - - - - - - - - - - - - - -

_____

_____

- - - - - - - - - - - - - - - - - - - - - - - - - - - - - - - -

_____

# Sensing the Season

_____

- - - - - - - - - - - - -

What season is it? _____
Use your senses to tell what's happening outside.

| I can **hear** | |
|---|---|
| I can **see** | |
| I can **touch** | |
| I can **taste** | |
| I can **smell** | |

# Sort These Recyclables

Draw a line from the picture to the recycle bin where it belongs.

1.

2.

3.

4.

5.

6.

7.

8.

PAPER

PLASTIC

GLASS

METAL

# Stop Air Pollution Now!

Here are three ways to prevent air pollution.  Color the pictures.
Talk about them with your friends.

**Compost Leaves
and Yard Waste**

**Ride Your Bike**

**Plant
Trees**

# I Can Make a Difference!

We all can make our world a better place!  Put a check mark by the things you can do to help our environment.

_____ Recycle paper, plastic, glass, and metal.

_____ Plant a flower or tree.

_____ Turn off lights to save energy.

_____ Use both sides of the paper.

_____ Never litter.

_____ Turn off the water when you brush your teeth.

_____ Ride your bike or walk to school.

_____ Compost leaves and yard waste.

# Math

These Math activities reinforce students' foundation for working with numbers. They will develop students' number sense with addition and subtraction, their ability to use basic operational math symbols and expressions, and their ability to describe common geometric shapes. Working through these activities will help them see that math has many practical applications on a daily basis and lays the foundation for making good lifelong economic decisions.

| Activity Title | Page | Content Standard and Skills Reinforced | EXTRA!  Extension Activities |
|---|---|---|---|
| How Many Dots? | 97 | Counting whole numbers | On a separate sheet of paper, have students create their own set of number cards using a symbol other than a dot. For example, they could use geometric shapes. Then have them write the number of shapes on each card. |
| Count the Flowers | 98 | Correlating numerals and number words up to 10 | Point out several things in the classroom. Write the number of the item on the board. Have students write the corresponding number word on the back of the activity sheet. |
| Count the Clouds | 99 | Correlating numerals and number words from 11 to 20 | Write number words on the board for 21 through 30. Have students write the corresponding numeral on the back of the activity sheet. |
| How Many in the Set? | 100 | •Sets  •Counting whole numbers  •Addition  •Multiple representation of the same number using a physical model | Prior to doing this activity with students, prepare several sets of items, such as pencils, crayons, pieces of chalk, or books. You may also draw sets on the board, or affix sets to the flannel board. Point out or hold up the items in each set, and have students pick up the number card or cards that equal the number of items. For example, if you hold up seven items, they could pick up the 1 card and the 6 card, or the 4 card and the 3 card. Point out how they are giving you different possibilities for arriving at the same answer. |
| Count by 2s | 101 | •Counting by 2s  •Recognizing patterns | Before handing out this activity, review how to count by 2s using common items in the class, or by counting off every other student. After you finish this activity, have students go row by row to continue the counting by twos, up to 30. |
| Count by 5s | 102 | •Counting by 5s using concrete objects  •Recognizing patterns | Before handing out this activity, review how to count by 5s. Once students put the cards in order, have them turn over their cards. Call out one number (example: 20) and have them call out what comes next, counting by 5. |
| Count by 10s | 103 | •Counting by 10s using concrete objects  •Recognizing patterns | Before handing out this activity, review how to count by 10s. Once students have put the cards in order, have them choose two cards from this deck—for example, 50 and 70. Have them count by 2s and 5s between each number. |
| Add Around the Wheel | 104 | Addition | Draw additional wheels on the board with different groups of numbers. Have students take turns coming up to the board and solving one problem of their choice in any of the wheels. |
| What's the Score? | 105 | Addition | Dictate additional strings of multiple numbers to students as they write them down and solve each problem. |
| How Many Carrots? | 106 | Addition with numbers up to 100 | Students may need a separate sheet of paper on which to write out their problems. Students may work in pairs. Or divide students into teams and have teams compete to complete each table first. |
| Subtract Around the Wheel | 107 | Subtraction | Draw additional wheels on the board with different groups of numbers. Have students take turns coming up to the board and solving one problem of their choice in any of the wheels. |
| Find the Message | 108 | Subtraction with numbers up to 100 | Write additional double-digit subtraction problems on the board for students to solve, or dictate problems and have students solve them on their papers. |
| Where Does the Dog Go? | 109 | •Addition  •Subtraction | Draw simple outlines of dogs on the board with answers only written in each dog. Have students generate addition or subtraction equations to fit each answer. You may wish to have students work in pairs. |

| Find the Difference | 110 | •Subtraction<br>•Deciding how to solve a problem | You may need to do this activity with the whole class. Point out that potential problems can be horizontal, vertical, backward, or forward. Reproduce additional puzzle pages like those shown for individual or group practice. |
|---|---|---|---|
| Dinosaurs | 111 | •Addition<br>•Subtraction<br>•Representing equivalent forms of the same number | Give students additional problems using the dinosaurs, or pinning numbers on things in the classroom, such as stuffed toys. |
| Color the Balloons | 112 | •Ordinal numbers<br>•Correlating ordinal numbers with cardinal numbers | Once students have finished this activity, work with them as a class to write the corresponding cardinal number under each balloon. |
| What Day Is It? | 113 | •Ordinal numbers<br>•Correlating ordinal numbers with cardinal numbers<br>•Reading a calendar | Remind students before they do this activity that Sunday is the first day of the week (even though we commonly think of Monday as the first day). After reviewing the activity, point out specific dates on your classroom calendar, such as Thanksgiving, and have students tell you what the day is in ordinal numbers. Example: "What day of the week is Thanksgiving?" |
| Shapes Jigsaw | 114 | Recognizing geometric shapes | Review with students some things that are round, triangular, oval, and rectangular. Depending on the level of your class, introduce more complex shapes, such as hexagons, pentagons, and diamonds. |
| Make a Picture! | 115 | Matching geometric shapes | Have students color their pictures. Display them on a class bulletin board. |
| More Than? Fewer Than? Equal To? | 116 | •Comparing two groups of 10 or fewer objects as having more, fewer, or the same number of objects<br>•Recognizing geometric shapes | Do this exercise with a variety of common objects, or continue the geometric shape theme. |
| Math Symbols | 117 | Mathematical symbols for more than, fewer or less than, and equal to | You may need to do this activity with the entire class. After you have finished, write pairs of numbers on the board. Have students write them on a separate piece of paper, inserting the greater than, less than, and equal to symbols as you dictate them. |
| Counting Change | 118 | •Recognizing coins<br>•Adding various denominations of coins | You may do this activity with the whole class and have students write the amounts in numbers under each set of coins. Pose real-life situations with which students are familiar—for example, buying milk in the cafeteria or buying things after school. Have them do similar problems. Example: "The milk in the cafeteria is 39¢. What coins could you use to pay for it?" |
| Circle the Symbol | 119 | •Adding denominations of coins<br>•Mathematical symbols for more than, fewer or less than, and equal to | Extend this activity by using real change and laying it out on a table for students to see. Put the change in two groups, as in the activity, and have the students count it out while you write the numbers on the board. Then subtract coins from each set you create and have students recalculate the number of coins in each set. |
| Do I Have Enough? | 120 | •Adding denominations of coins<br>•Setting up a simple problem<br>•Recognizing the cent sign | Review with students how to set up problems. Review each item in this activity. Have students tell you how they set up the problem and how much more money they need if they do not have enough. Show each problem in a simple equation. |
| Help the Mouse Draw the Time | 121 | •Telling time to the half-hour and to the hour<br>•Terms related to telling time | After you review the activity, review drawing time to the quarter hour. Draw additional clocks on the board. |
| What Time Does It Happen? | 122 | •Associating clock time with real time<br>•Writing the time<br>•Using AM and PM | Give students additional times to draw. Example: "When is your favorite TV show? What time do you get up on Saturday? What time do you go to bed on Friday night?" |
| What Tool Should I Use? | 123 | Using the appropriate tool to measure length, time, temperature, and weight | Show additional things in the classroom that would be weighed or measured, and ask students what tool they would use to do so. |
| Crack the Code! | 124 | Number to letter association | Depending on the level of your students, you may need to do this activity with the entire class. Using the same number to letter correlation, have students create their own secret messages and then switch papers with each other to solve the messages. |

# How Many Dots?

How many dots are on each card?  Write the number of dots below each card.

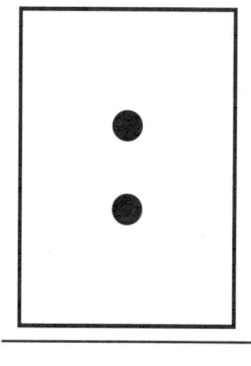

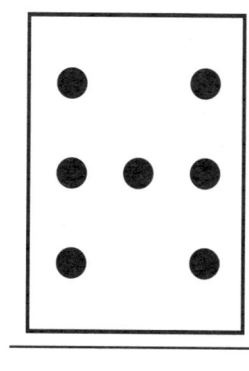

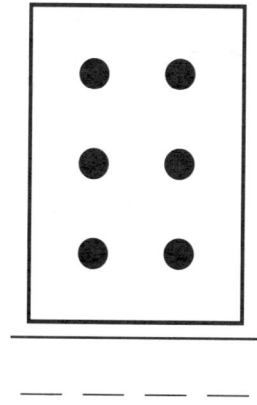

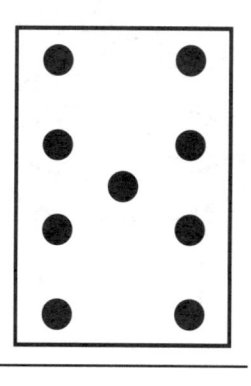

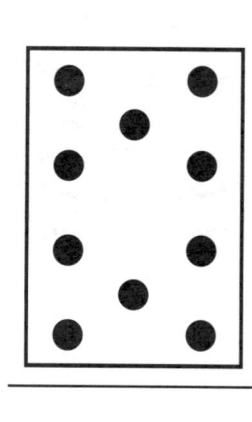

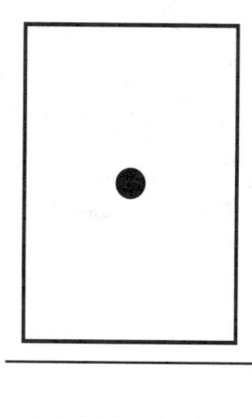

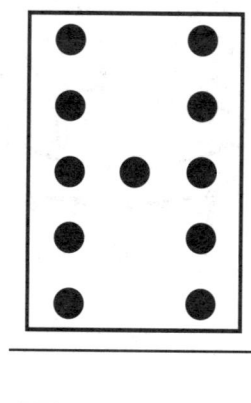

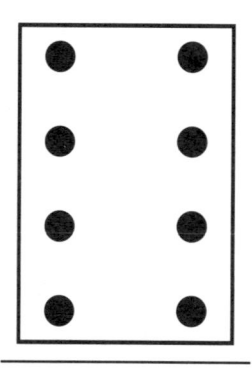

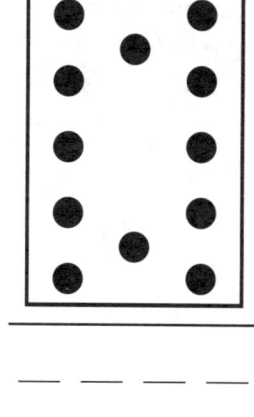

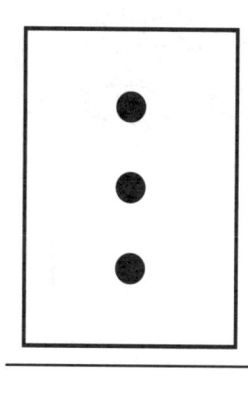

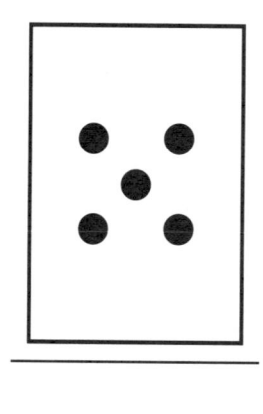

# Count the Flowers

Write the word for the number of flowers in each pot.

 8

 6

 1

 2

_ _ _ _ _ _ _ _ _ _ _ _ _ _ _ _ _ _ _ _ _ _ _ _

_____

 4

 5

 7

 3

_ _ _ _ _ _ _ _ _ _ _ _ _ _ _ _ _ _ _ _ _ _ _ _

_____

 9

 10

_ _ _ _ _ _     _ _ _ _ _ _

_____     _____

Name _____     Date _____

# Count the Clouds

Write the correct number on each cloud.

| 11 | 12 | 13 | 14 | 15 | 16 | 17 | 18 | 19 | 20 |

sixteen

eighteen

twelve

fourteen

twenty

seventeen

eleven

nineteen

fifteen

thirteen

# How Many in the Set?

Cut out each number card.  Lay it on your desk.  Pick up the card or cards that show how many things are in each set your teacher shows you.

- - - - - - - - ✂ - - - - - - - - - - - - - - - - - - - - - - - -

| | | |
|---|---|---|
| 1 | 2 | 3 |
| 4 | 5 | 6 |

# Count by 2s

Mark an **X** on the wrong number in each row.  Write the correct number in the box.

| | | | | | | |
|---|---|---|---|---|---|---|
| 2 | 4 | 5 | 8 | 10 | 12 | _____ |
| 1 | 3 | 4 | 7 | 9 | 11 | _____ |
| 5 | 7 | 9 | 11 | 13 | 16 | _____ |
| 10 | 12 | 14 | 15 | 18 | 20 | _____ |
| 1 | 4 | 6 | 8 | 10 | 12 | _____ |
| 9 | 11 | 13 | 14 | 17 | 19 | _____ |

# Count by 5s

Cut out the number cards.  Put the cards on your desk in order.
Start with 5.

✂ - - - - - - - - - - - - - - - - - - - - - - - - - - - - - - - -

| | | |
|---|---|---|
| **5** | **25** | **15** |
| **20** | **10** | **30** |

# Count by 10s

Cut out the number cards.  Put the cards on your desk in order.
Start with 10.

--------- ✂ ------------------------------------

| | | | |
|---|---|---|---|
| **50** | **100** | **20** | **70** |
| **30** | **40** | **10** | **80** |
| | **60** | **90** | |

Math

# Add Around the Wheel

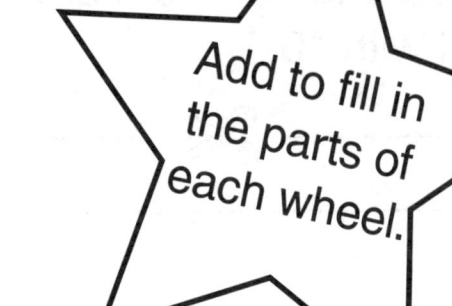

Add to fill in the parts of each wheel.

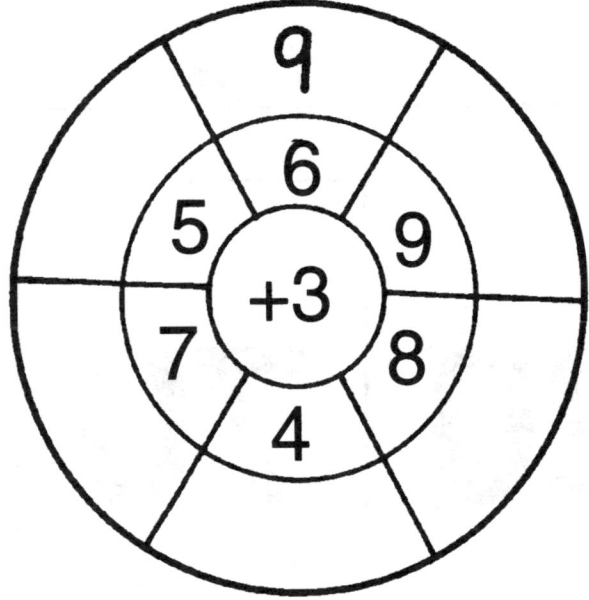

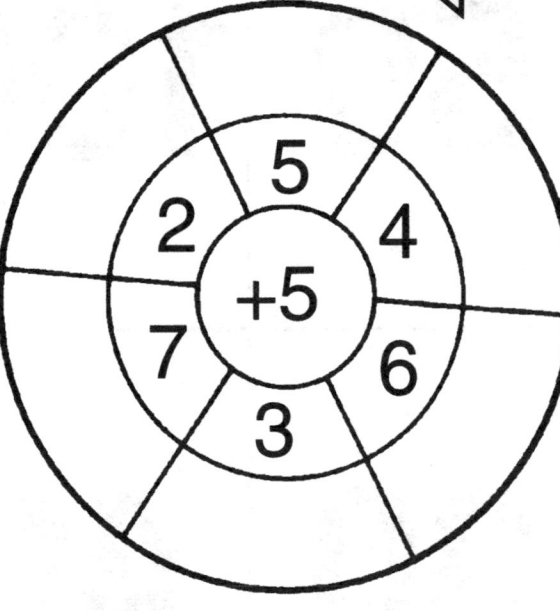

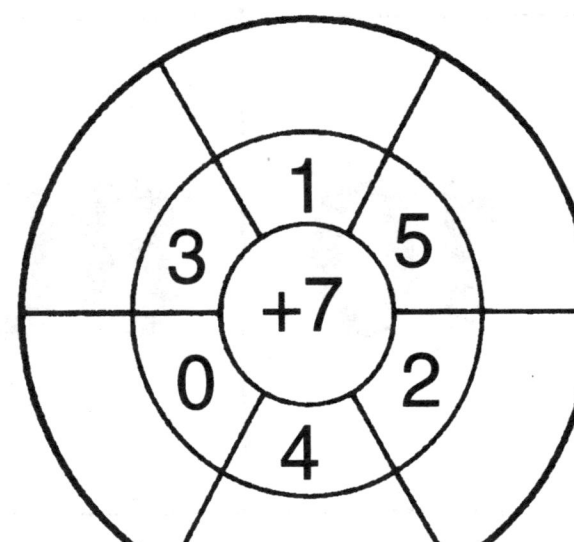

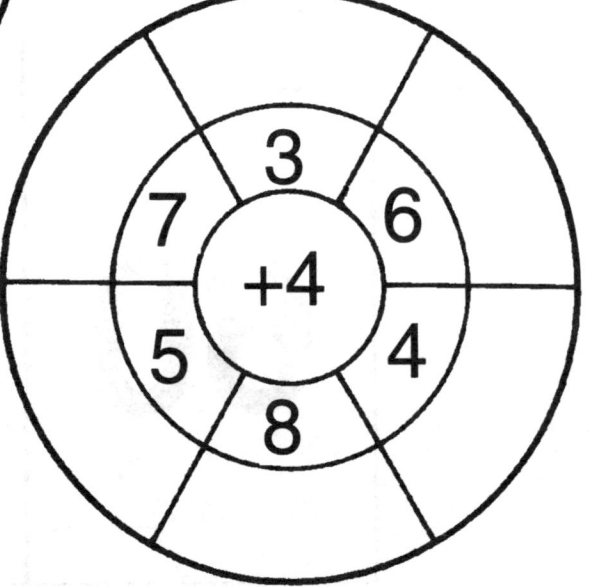

# What's the Score?

Add the scores of each game.  Circle the winners.

**GAME 1**

| | | | | | | | | | | |
|---|---|---|---|---|---|---|---|---|---|---|
| Home | 0 | 1 | 3 | 0 | 0 | 0 | 5 | 0 | 0 | |
| Visitors | 2 | 0 | 1 | 0 | 2 | 0 | 0 | 0 | 1 | |

**GAME 2**

| | | | | | | | | | | |
|---|---|---|---|---|---|---|---|---|---|---|
| Cards | 1 | 0 | 0 | 0 | 1 | 2 | 0 | 0 | 0 | |
| Cubs | 0 | 2 | 2 | 0 | 0 | 0 | 0 | 0 | 1 | |

**GAME 3**

| | | | | | | | | | | |
|---|---|---|---|---|---|---|---|---|---|---|
| Giants | 3 | 0 | 3 | 0 | 0 | 0 | 0 | 1 | 0 | |
| Reds | 0 | 5 | 1 | 0 | 1 | 1 | 0 | 0 | 0 | |

**GAME 4**

| | | | | | | | | | | |
|---|---|---|---|---|---|---|---|---|---|---|
| Astros | 0 | 0 | 0 | 4 | 1 | 2 | 0 | 0 | 3 | |
| Dodgers | 2 | 0 | 3 | 2 | 1 | 0 | 0 | 0 | 1 | |

**GAME 5**

| | | | | | | | | | | |
|---|---|---|---|---|---|---|---|---|---|---|
| Giants | 4 | 2 | 0 | 0 | 1 | 5 | 0 | 0 | 0 | |
| Cubs | 0 | 1 | 3 | 0 | 0 | 0 | 5 | 0 | 0 | |

**GAME 6**

| | | | | | | | | | | |
|---|---|---|---|---|---|---|---|---|---|---|
| Reds | 0 | 0 | 0 | 2 | 0 | 4 | 0 | 0 | 0 | |
| Pirates | 4 | 0 | 0 | 0 | 3 | 1 | 0 | 0 | 0 | |

**GAME 7**

| | | | | | | | | | | |
|---|---|---|---|---|---|---|---|---|---|---|
| Phillies | 0 | 1 | 5 | 3 | 2 | 0 | 0 | 0 | 1 | |
| Cubs | 0 | 0 | 0 | 0 | 6 | 5 | 0 | 0 | 0 | |

MP5105

Math

Name _____     Date _____

# How Many Carrots?

Complete each table.

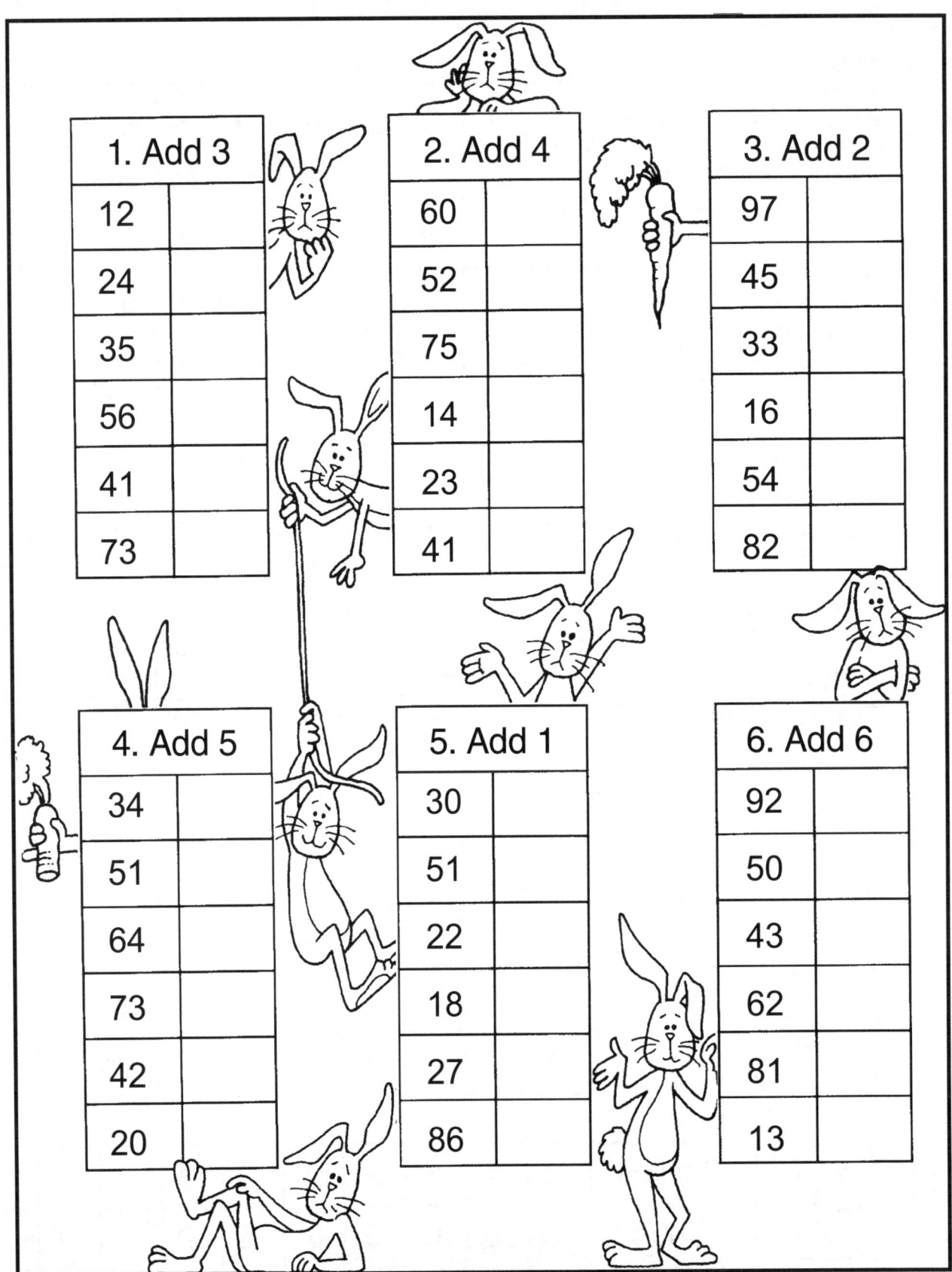

| 1. Add 3 | |
|---|---|
| 12 | |
| 24 | |
| 35 | |
| 56 | |
| 41 | |
| 73 | |

| 2. Add 4 | |
|---|---|
| 60 | |
| 52 | |
| 75 | |
| 14 | |
| 23 | |
| 41 | |

| 3. Add 2 | |
|---|---|
| 97 | |
| 45 | |
| 33 | |
| 16 | |
| 54 | |
| 82 | |

| 4. Add 5 | |
|---|---|
| 34 | |
| 51 | |
| 64 | |
| 73 | |
| 42 | |
| 20 | |

| 5. Add 1 | |
|---|---|
| 30 | |
| 51 | |
| 22 | |
| 18 | |
| 27 | |
| 86 | |

| 6. Add 6 | |
|---|---|
| 92 | |
| 50 | |
| 43 | |
| 62 | |
| 81 | |
| 13 | |

MP5105

Math

# Subtract Around the Wheel

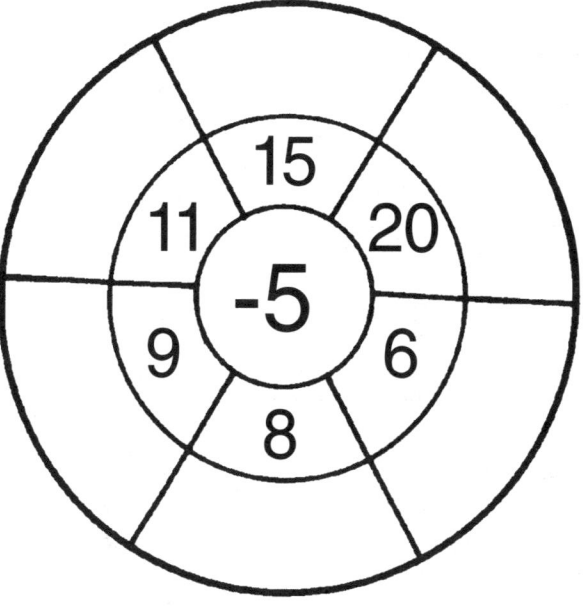

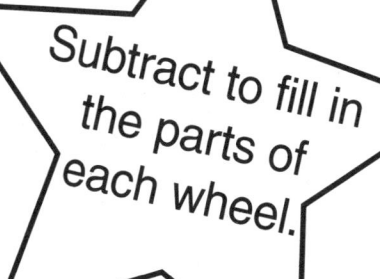

Subtract to fill in the parts of each wheel.

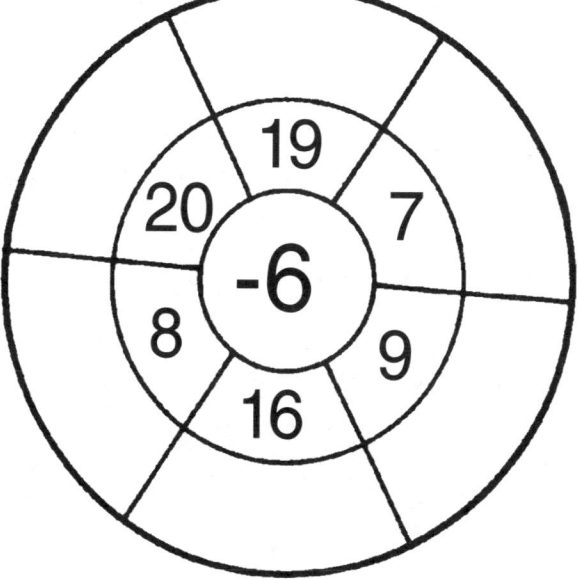

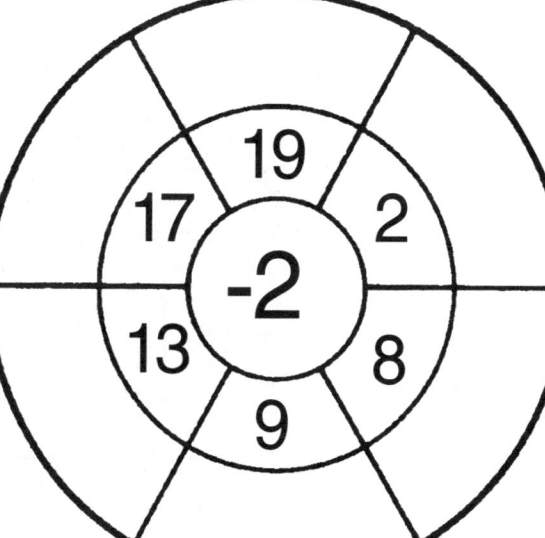

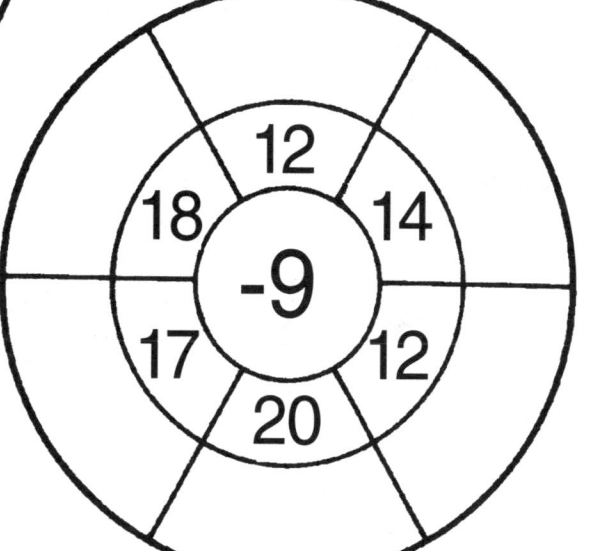

# Find the Message

Complete the problems.  Write the letter for the answer under each problem.

| 21 | 22 | 43 | 56 | 61 | 78 | 34 | 51 | 75 | 42 | 40 | 32 | 23 | 35 |
|----|----|----|----|----|----|----|----|----|----|----|----|----|----|
| H | S | A | U | N | E | M | O | C | G | D | T | P | W |

| 78<br>− 43 | 38<br>− 17 | 99<br>− 56 | 55<br>− 23 | 79<br>− 37 | 83<br>− 32 | 89<br>− 11 | 42<br>− 20 |
|---|---|---|---|---|---|---|---|
| ☐ | ☐ | ☐ | ☐ | ☐ | ☐ | ☐ | ☐ |

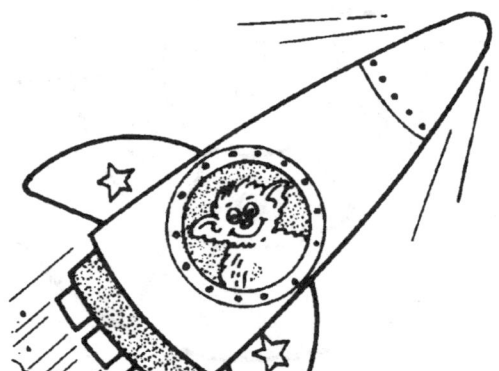

| 77<br>− 21 | 84<br>− 61 |
|---|---|
| ☐ | ☐ |

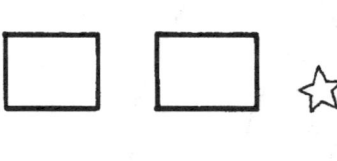

| 99<br>− 65 | 88<br>− 32 | 56<br>− 34 | 77<br>− 45 | 87<br>− 12 | 67<br>− 16 | 86<br>− 52 | 98<br>− 20 |
|---|---|---|---|---|---|---|---|
| ☐ | ☐ | ☐ | ☐ | ☐ | ☐ | ☐ | ☐ |

| 68<br>− 28 | 97<br>− 46 | 77<br>− 42 | 94<br>− 33 |
|---|---|---|---|
| ☐ | ☐ | ☐ | ☐ |

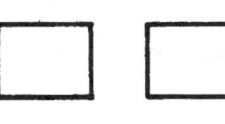

# Where Does the Dog Go?

Name _____

Add the numbers on each doghouse.
Cut out the dogs, and glue them under the correct doghouses.

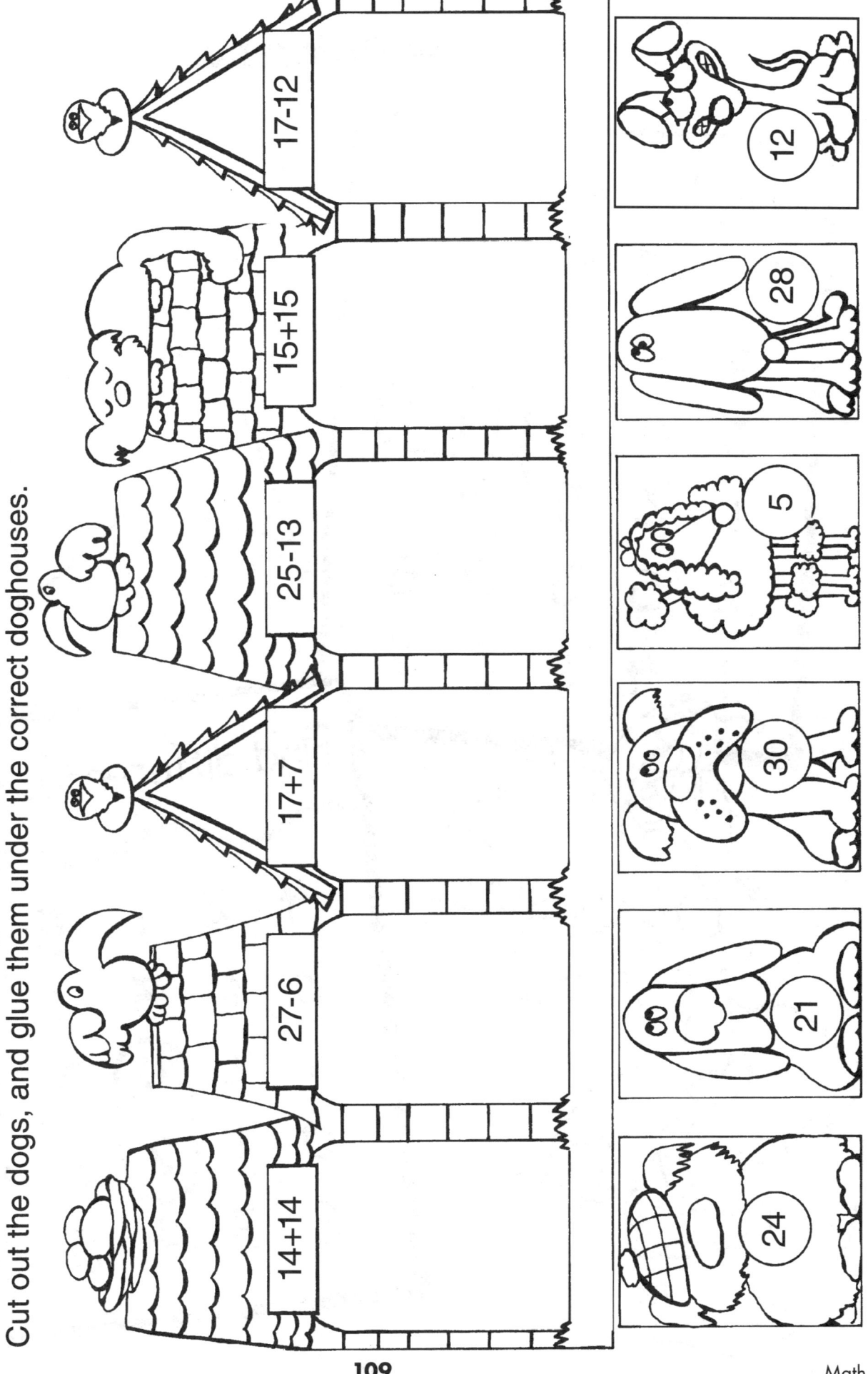

Doghouses: 17-12, 15+15, 25-13, 17+7, 27-6, 14+14

Dogs: 12, 28, 5, 30, 21, 24

# Find the Difference

### Find differences of 3...

| 6 | 1 | 4 | 3 | 0 |
|---|---|---|---|---|
| 3 | 0 | 2 | 1 | 4 |
| 1 | 3 | 5 | 4 | 0 |
| 2 | 5 | 3 | 0 | 5 |
| 1 | 4 | 6 | 6 | 2 |

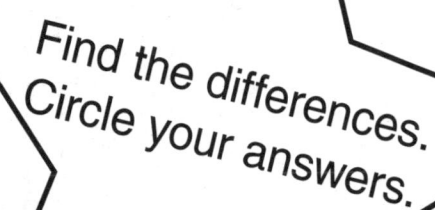

Find the differences.
Circle your answers.

### Find differences of 2...

| 4 | 2 | 1 | 5 | 3 |
|---|---|---|---|---|
| 3 | 0 | 3 | 1 | 4 |
| 1 | 6 | 4 | 3 | 5 |
| 0 | 1 | 2 | 3 | 4 |
| 2 | 3 | 4 | 5 | 6 |

# Dinosaurs

Write a math problem that equals the answer in each dinosaur.  You can write an addition or subtraction problem.

# Color the Balloons

1. Color the **third** balloon **orange**.

2. Color the **sixth** balloon **blue**.

3. Color the **second** balloon **green**.

4. Color the **ninth** balloon **red**.

5. Color the **first** balloon **brown**.

6. Color the **fourth** balloon **purple**.

7. Color the **eighth** balloon **yellow**.

8. Color the **fifth** balloon **black**.

9. Color the **tenth** balloon **green and blue**.

10. Color the **seventh** balloon **brown and orange**.

# What Day Is It?

## NOVEMBER

| Sunday | Monday | Tuesday | Wednesday | Thursday | Friday | Saturday |
|--------|--------|---------|-----------|----------|--------|----------|
| 1 | 2 | 3 | 4 | 5 | 6 | 7 |
| 8 | 9 | 10 | 11 | 12 | 13 | 14 |
| 15 | 16 | 17 | 18 | 19 | 20 | 21 |
| 22 | 23 | 24 | 25 | 26 | 27 | 28 |
| 29 | 30 | | | | | |

1. Color the **first** day of the **second** week **red**.

2. Color the **second** day of the **last** week **orange**.

3. Color the **fifth** day of the **third** week **yellow**.

4. Color the **sixth** day of the **fourth** week **green**.

5. Color the **fifth** day of the **second** week **blue**.

6. Color the **fourth** day of the **second** week **purple**.

7. Color the **third** day of the **first** week **pink**.

8. Color the **seventh** day of the **second** week **brown**.

# Shapes Jigsaw

Cut out each puzzle piece.  Fit them together to make a shape.
(Hint: There are puzzle pieces for four shapes.)

✂ - - - - - - - - - - - - - - - - - - - - - - - - - - - - - - - - - - - - -

Name _____  Date _____

# Make a Picture!

Cut out the shapes at the bottom of the page.  Glue them to the shapes at the top of the page.

What did you make? _____

✂ - - - - - - - - - - - - - - - - - - - - - - - - - - - - - - - - - - - - - - - -

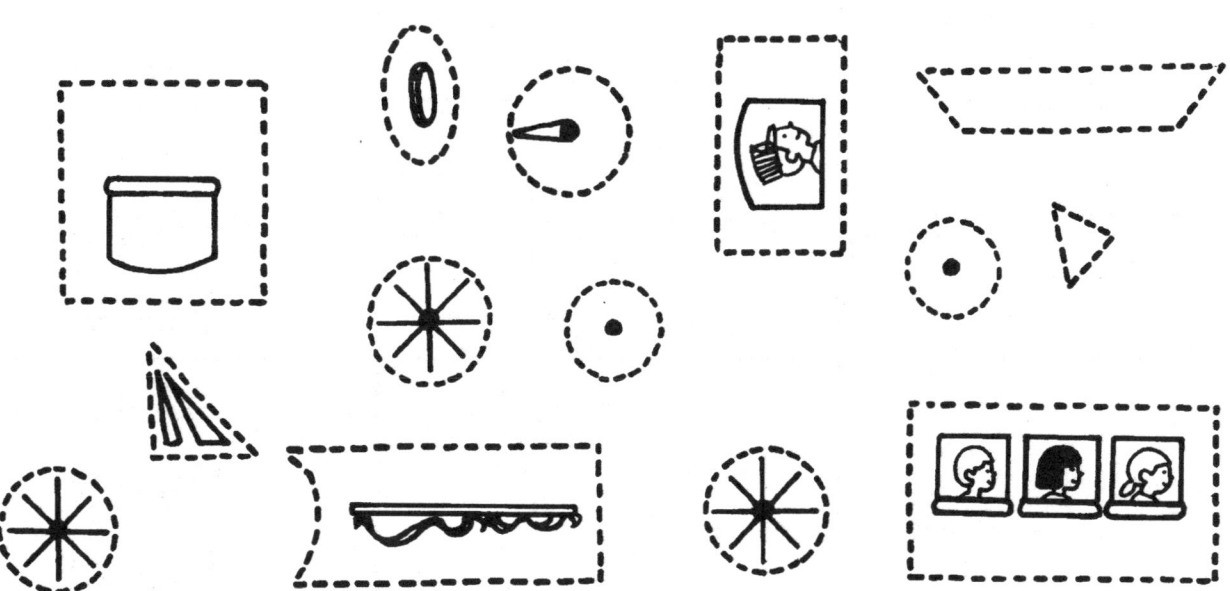

# More Than?  Fewer Than?  Equal To?

Look at the second group of pictures.  Are there more, fewer, or an equal number?  Circle the correct word.

| | | |
|---|---|---|
| | | More<br>Fewer<br>Equal |
| | | More<br>Fewer<br>Equal |
| | | More<br>Fewer<br>Equal |
| | | More<br>Fewer<br>Equal |
| | | More<br>Fewer<br>Equal |
| | | More<br>Fewer<br>Equal |

# Math Symbols

In math, we can use symbols to show greater than, fewer or less than, or equal to.

| Symbol | Example Using Symbols | Example Using Words |
|--------|----------------------|---------------------|
| > | 7 > 2 | 7 is greater than 2 |
| < | 10 < 12 | 10 is less than 12 |
| = | 8 = 8 | 8 is equal to 8 |

Fill in this chart. Rewrite each example using symbols instead of words.

| | |
|---|---|
| 18 is less than 20 | 18 < 20 |
| 12 is more than 11 | |
| 30 is more than 28 | |
| 18 is less than 29 | |
| 23 is equal to 23 | |
| 20 is more than 8 | |
| 25 is less than 26 | |
| 9 is equal to 9 | |
| 1 is less than 10 | |
| 6 is equal to 6 | |
| 17 is less than 21 | |

# Counting Change

Add the change shown.

**1.**

= _ _ _ _

**2.**

= _ _ _ _

**3.**

= _ _ _ _

**4.**

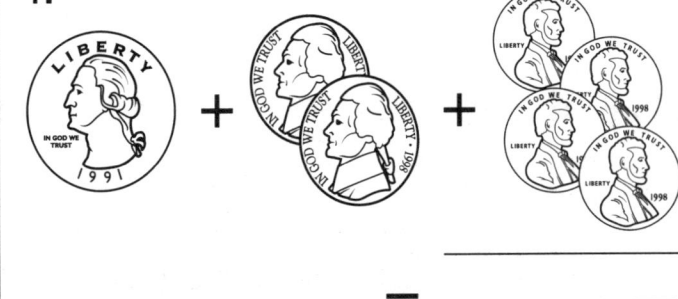

= _ _ _ _

**5.**

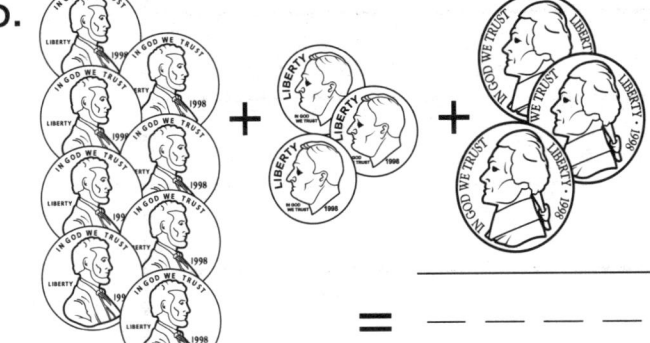

= _ _ _ _

**6.**

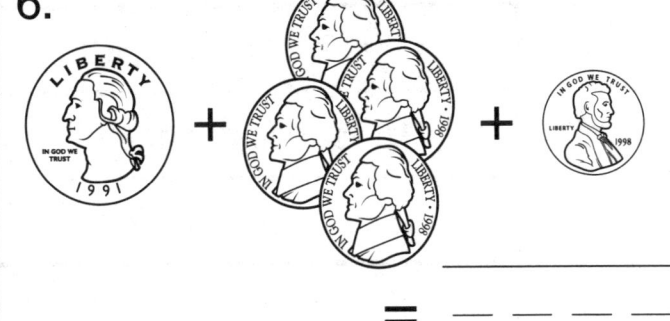

= _ _ _ _

**7.**

= _ _ _ _

**8.**

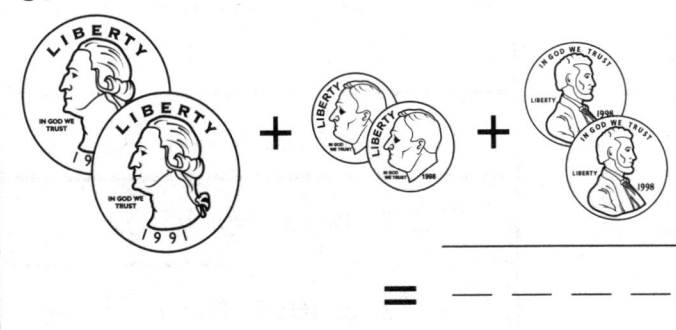

= _ _ _ _

# Circle the Symbol

How much money is in the left box? How much money is in the right box? Circle the correct math symbol between each box.

| | | | |
|---|---|---|---|
| 1. | | > <br> < <br> = | |
| 2. | | > <br> < <br> = | |
| 3. | | > <br> < <br> = | |
| 4. | | > <br> < <br> = | |
| 5. | | > <br> < <br> = | |
| 6. | | > <br> < <br> = | |

# Do I Have Enough?

Do you have enough to buy each item?  Circle **YES** or **NO**.

1. A banana is 30¢.  You have  .

   Do you have enough money to buy the banana?          **YES    NO**

2. A pack of crayons is 89¢.  You have  .

   Do you have enough money to buy the crayons?          **YES    NO**

3. A coloring book is 65¢.  You have .

   Do you have enough money to buy the coloring book?      **YES    NO**

4. A can of fruit juice is 40¢.  You have .

   Do you have enough money to buy the fruit juice?          **YES    NO**

5. A package of flower seeds is 99¢.  You have .

   Do you have enough money to buy the seeds?          **YES    NO**

# Help the Mouse Draw the Time

Help the mouse draw the time on each of these clocks.

1.

Show 6:00.

2.

Show 4:30.

3.

Show 9:30.

4.

Show 1:00.

5.

Show 2:30.

6.

Show 5:30.

7.

Show 12:30.

8.

Show 7:00.

9.

Show 3:30.

# What Time Does It Happen?

Answer each question by drawing the time on the clock. Then write the time next to each clock. Be sure to use A.M. or P.M. when you write each time.

1. What time do you leave for school?

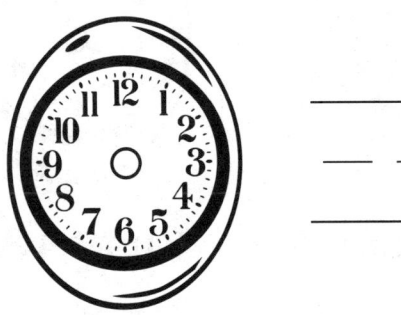

_____

_ _ _ _

_____

2. What time does school start?

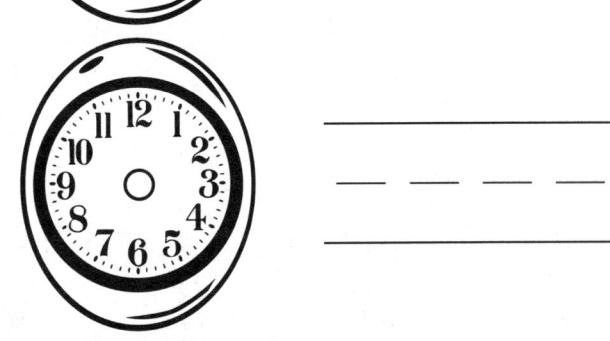

_____

_ _ _ _

_____

3. What time do we go to lunch?

_____

_ _ _ _

_____

4. What time is it now?

_____

_ _ _ _

_____

5. What time do we go home?

_____

_ _ _ _

_____

# What Tool Should I Use?

Write which tool you would use to measure each of the following.

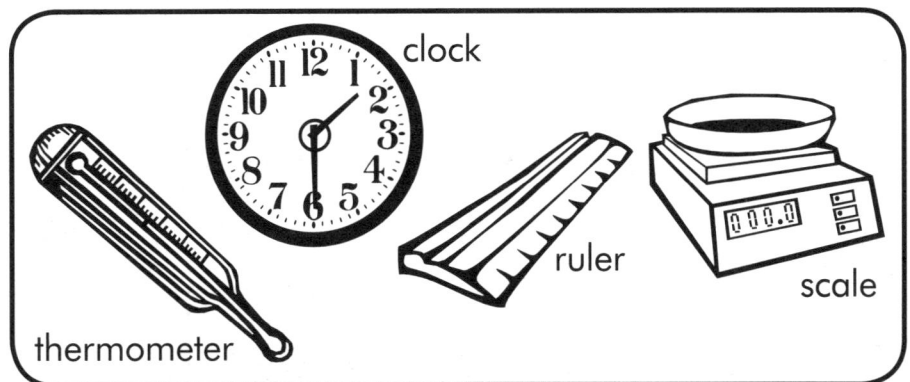

clock

ruler

scale

thermometer

**1.**

The weight of a bag of apples.

\_ \_ \_ \_ \_ \_ \_ \_ \_

**2.**

The temperature on a rainy day.

\_ \_ \_ \_ \_ \_ \_ \_ \_

**3.**

The length of your shoelaces.

\_ \_ \_ \_ \_ \_ \_ \_ \_

**4.**

The time to go to school.

\_ \_ \_ \_ \_ \_ \_ \_ \_

**5.**

The weight of a pumpkin.

\_ \_ \_ \_ \_ \_ \_ \_ \_

**6.**

The length of a piece of paper.

\_ \_ \_ \_ \_ \_ \_ \_ \_

**7.**

The time for your favorite TV program.

\_ \_ \_ \_ \_ \_ \_ \_ \_

**8.**

If your snowman will melt.

\_ \_ \_ \_ \_ \_ \_ \_ \_

**9.**

If its warm enough to plant flowers.

\_ \_ \_ \_ \_ \_ \_ \_ \_

**10.**

Your dog's weight.

\_ \_ \_ \_ \_ \_ \_ \_ \_

# Crack the Code!

Here's an easy way to create a secret code!  Give each letter of the alphabet a different number.  Then use numbers for letters.

| | | | | |
|---|---|---|---|---|
| A=1 | B=2 | C=3 | D=4 | E=5 |
| F=6 | G=7 | H=8 | I=9 | J=10 |
| K=11 | L=12 | M=13 | N=14 | O=15 |
| P=16 | Q=17 | R=18 | S=19 | T=20 |
| U=21 | V=22 | W=23 | X=24 | Y=25 |
| Z=26 | | | | |

***Example:***

8   15   23      1   18   5      25   15   21

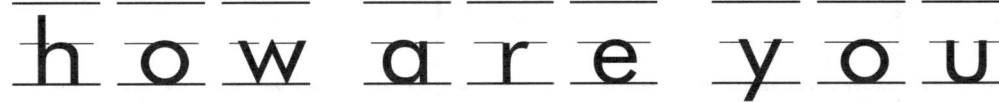

13   1   20   8      9   19      6   21   14

___   ___   ___   ___      ___   ___      ___   ___   ___

9   3   1   14      20   5   12   12      20   9   13   5

___   ___   ___   ___      ___   ___   ___   ___      ___   ___   ___   ___

1   4   4   9   14   7      9   19      5   1   19   25

___   ___   ___   ___   ___   ___      ___   ___      ___   ___   ___   ___

# Answer Key

## Language Arts

### Spelling Word Scramble (page 10)

1. light
2. house
3. yellow
4. little
5. down
6. friend
7. always
8. jump

### Make New Words (page 17)

1. doorbell
2. cupcake
3. basketball
4. snowman
5. football
6. butterfly
7. cowboy
8. toothbrush

### What Comes Next? (page 23)

*Row 1:* 3, 1, 2
*Row 2:* 1, 3, 2
*Row 3:* 2, 1, 3

### Solve the Mystery (page 25)

*Story 1:* Kamal went to the wrong house. He got confused because all of the houses on the street look alike.
*Story 2:* Mr. Kim pulled the wrong coat from the coat rack.

### Tanya's Furry Gift (page 32)

Today was Tanya's big day! It was her **sixth** birthday. Her dad was going to take her to the pet **store**. They were going to pick out a puppy. Tanya went down to breakfast. Her mom had fixed her favorite **breakfast**. Tanya began to eat. But her throat **hurt**. She felt hot. "You're not well!" said her mom. "You should go back to bed." So Tanya did. A little later, she woke up. Something **warm** and **furry** (or furry and warm) was licking her **face**. Her dad stood at the end of her bed. "Happy birthday, Tanya!" he said. "Do you like your new **puppy**?" Tanya happily hugged the puppy.

# Social Studies

## Urban, Rural, or Suburban (page 40)

1. rural
2. suburban
3. urban
4. rural
5. rural
6. urban
7. suburban
8. urban

## What Did You Say? (page 44)

1. D
2. E
3. G
4. F
5. J
6. I
7. B
8. C
9. A
10. H

## North, South, East, or West? (page 48)

1. north
2. west
3. south
4. east
5. west

## United States Holidays (page 51)

1. D
2. F
3. E
4. C
5. B
6. A

## The United States Flag (page 52)

1. false
2. true
3. true
4. true
5. false

## American Landmarks Word Search (page 58)

```
C  F  H  J  X  N  V  C  T  R
W  A  G  A  T  E  W  A  Y  U
A  V  G  R  I  E  O  P  U  S
S  P  A  C  E  D  V  I  L  H
H  B  Q  H  P  L  V  T  L  M
I  X  Z  S  M  E  J  O  L  O
N  P  L  I  N  C  O  L  N  R
G  O  L  D  E  N  X  Z  M  E
T  A  S  Q  U  I  O  V  C  F
O  S  M  P  A  K  X  P  X  H
N  P  S  A  B  R  I  D  G  E
```

## Famous American Inventors (page 60)

1. Henry Ford
2. Eli Whitney
3. Alexander Graham Bell
4. Thomas Edison
5. George Washington Carver
6. Wilbur and Orville Wright

## Goods or Services? (page 61)

1. goods
2. goods (bicycles) and services (bicycle repair)
3. service
4. service
5. service
6. service
7. goods (pets and pet supplies) and services (pet grooming, pet training)
8. service
9. service
10. service

## Producers or Consumers? (page 62)

1. consumer
2. producer
3. producers
4. producer
5. consumer
6. consumer
7. producer
8. producer
9. producer
10. producer

# Science

## Solid, Liquid, or Gas? (page 67)

*Solids:* pencil, leaf, seashell
*Liquids:* water, juice, milk
*Gases:* helium, hydrogen, oxygen

## What Plants Give Us (page 73)

1. food
2. nest
3. shade
4. rope
5. cotton
6. soap

## Frog Life Cycle (page 79)

*#1 in cycle:* Eggs
*#2 in cycle:* Tiny tadpoles with tail
*#3 in cycle:* Growing tadpole with legs and small tail
*#4 in cycle:* More fully formed frog with larger eyes and mouth than tadpole; smaller tail
*#5 in cycle:* Fully formed frog

## Weather Words (page 85)

1. breeze
2. air
3. dew
4. barometer
5. freeze
6. frost
7. smog
8. humidity
9. clouds
10. fog

## Types of Clouds (page 88)

*cirrus clouds:* thin, wispy
*stratus clouds:* gray like fog, look like flat sheets
*cumulus clouds:* white and puffy, flat bases and lumpy tops

# Math

## What's the Score? (page 105)

Game 1:  9 to 6
Game 2:  4 to 5
Game 3:  7 to 8
Game 4:  10 to 9
Game 5:  12 to 9
Game 6:  6 to 8
Game 7:  12 to 11

## How Many Carrots? (page 106)

1. Add 3:  15, 27, 38, 59, 44, 76
2. Add 4:  64, 56, 79, 18, 27, 45
3. Add 2: 99, 47, 35, 18, 56, 84
4. Add 5:  39, 56, 69, 78, 47, 25
5. Add 1:  31, 52, 23, 19, 28, 87
6. Add 6:  98, 56, 49, 68, 87, 19

## Find the Message (page 108)

What goes up must come down

## Find the Difference (page 110)

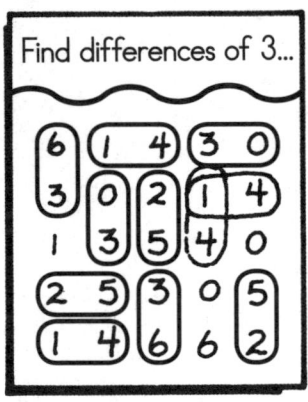
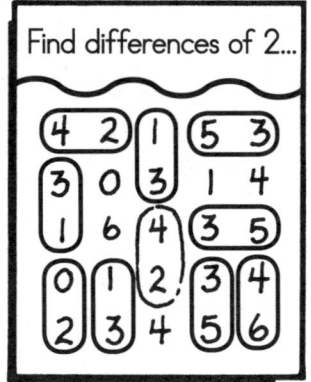

## What Day Is It? (page 113)

*Dates that should be colored for each numbered item:*

1. November 8
2. November 30
3. November 19
4. November 27
5. November 12
6. November 11
7. November 3
8. November 14

## Counting Change (page 118)

1. 18¢
2. 46¢
3. 16¢
4. 39¢
5. 53¢
6. 46¢
7. 64¢
8. 72¢

## Circle the Symbol (page 119)

1. less than
2. equal to
3. greater than
4. equal to
5. equal to
6. less than

## Do I Have Enough? (page 120)

1. no
2. no
3. no
4. yes
5. yes

## Crack the Code (page 124)

1. Math is fun
2. I can tell time
3. Adding is easy